Story Writing

Master the Fundamentals of Unforgettable Stories

(A Practical Guide to Writing Stories That Win Contests and Get Selected for Publication)

John Estell

Published By **Bella Frost**

John Estell

All Rights Reserved

Story Writing: Master the Fundamentals of Unforgettable Stories (A Practical Guide to Writing Stories That Win Contests and Get Selected for Publication)

ISBN 978-1-77485-941-4

No part of this guidebook shall be reproduced in any form without permission in writing from the publisher except in the case of brief quotations embodied in critical articles or reviews.

Legal & Disclaimer

The information contained in this ebook is not designed to replace or take the place of any form of medicine or professional medical advice. The information in this ebook has been provided for educational & entertainment purposes only.

The information contained in this book has been compiled from sources deemed reliable, and it is accurate to the best of the Author's knowledge; however, the Author cannot guarantee its accuracy and validity and cannot be held liable for any errors or omissions. Changes are periodically made to this book. You must consult your doctor or get professional medical advice before using any of the suggested remedies, techniques, or information in this book.

Upon using the information contained in this book, you agree to hold harmless the Author from and against any damages, costs, and expenses, including any legal fees potentially resulting from the application of any of the information provided by this guide. This disclaimer applies to any damages or injury caused by the use and application, whether directly or indirectly, of any advice or information presented, whether for breach of contract, tort, negligence, personal injury, criminal intent, or under any other cause of action.

You agree to accept all risks of using the information presented inside this book. You need to consult a professional medical practitioner in order to ensure you are both able and healthy enough to participate in this program.

Table of contents

Chapter 1: Getting Started 1

Chapter 2: Getting Good At Writing Log Lines.. 7

Chapter 3: Finding Inspiration................. 13

Chapter 4: Generating Ideas 30

Chapter 5: Greek Mythology................... 38

Chapter 6: Give Someone The Shake ... 118

Chapter 7: Using Free Writing.............. 139

Chapter 8: Getting Moving................... 172

Chapter 1: GETTING STARTED

How To Use This Book

This book can be read straight through or you can skip to the sections that make the most sense for you. Each of the topics under the GENERATING IDEAS section includes an exercise for you to try yourself!

I advise reading the entire book once and trying every exercise, then bookmarking the ones that work for you and focus only on those. But keep in mind—next time you need to come up with a novel idea, a different strategy might work better for that project than the one that worked for this one!

Good luck!

Arming Yourself With The Right Tools

Before you get starting generating killer book ideas, you want to make sure you're prepared to do so. I use a variety of tools and skills to make collecting and analyzing my ideas easier. Here are the ones that make my life easier. Of course, these may not work for you. The key here is to choose something that does.

TOOLS

1. Something to Keep With You At All Times

Maybe this is a physical notebook you store in your purse or an app on your phone (my preferred method) but you want to make sure you have a tool at the ready to jot down ideas as they come to you. I often do a lot of my idea generation and brainstorming on my morning train commute or in the car. I keep my phone in my lap with the Notepad or an equivalent app open to write down ideas as I discover them. Once I'm back at my computer, I'll organize the ideas into a file so they are all in one place. I've even heard of people sticking a waterproof notebook inside their showers.

2. Evernote

Evernote is a program that can be synced on multiple devices (such as computer and phone). You store notes in separate groups called "Notebooks" and have individual "Notes" within each Notebook. For example, I might have a Notebook called "Book Ideas" and each fragment of an idea I have goes into a separate Note. Once I start fleshing out the plot a bit more, I might turn the idea into another Notebook for that idea only to organize my ideas for individual chapters or to capture research.

For example, an idea note in my "Book Ideas" folder might say something really generic like "Sibling rivalry that goes too far." But as I mull over that topic, I realize I have a few additional ideas to tack onto that specific idea. I start adding them into the same Note file so it begins to look like:

• Sibling rivalry that goes too far

• Could be about two sisters vying for the same goal

• Maybe one sister does something unforgivable to the other

- Setting could be someplace where they're trapped with each other and forced to reconcile

As I start jotting down ideas, the novel begins to take shape so I move it into its own Notebook called "Sisters Novel." Within that, I create separate Notes for each aspect of the above. For example:

Note title: Vying for the same goal

Body of Note:

- Competition they both enter? Dance?

- Same boy?

- Maybe one of them is more skilled than the other and this causes jealousy

Note title: One sister does something unforgivable

Body of Note:

- Steals boyfriend?

- Nah, cliche. Maybe instead they date brothers.

- Cheats during competition?

- Maybe she doesn't cheat but instead she steals the glory from the sister who deserved it by winning as an underdog.

- Permanently injures her sister?

- Maybe this could be a mystery. Reader knows at the start an injury occurred and Sister 1 is at fault but the novel then goes on to reveal how and why it happened.

Note title: Setting Ideas

Body of Note:

- Cruise

- Stuck in same, tiny cabin. Claustrophobic.

- Prison together?

- Nah, this would result in a different kind of novel

How I jotted each individual idea above is something I'll talk through in the Generating Ideas section. Evernote is also great at saving research into the same Notebook and keeping everything in one place. There's a plugin for your browser and phone. With one click you can save a website into the notebook to refer back to later. In the above scenario (which became my YA novel KASEY SCREWS UP THE WORLD), I saved a lot of research about dance, cruises, permanent hip injuries, etc.

3. GoogleDocs

An alternative to Evernote is using GoogleDocs, which is also accessible from the Internet on any device. Word documents work as well. Scrivener too. I also sometimes use Excel. The point is to find the tool that works best for YOU and then stick with that method.

Chapter 2: Getting Good At Writing Log Lines

In order to begin generating ideas, you need to be able to write a log line. A log line is simply a one sentence description of your book that highlights the main conflict. Think of the log line as the answer to the question, "What is your book about?" You need to be able to explain the plot in a single sentence. Bonus points if your sentence makes the audience go, "oooh! I want to read that!" That's called a hook.

A hook is the part of the idea that's unique and makes people instantly want to read it.

A simple log line formula: who is the main character + what the main character wants + what's standing in their way of getting it. Some people also add a ticking clock factor or an "or else" factor to give it an extra twist.

For example, let's look at a story and try to identify the above. We'll use OCEAN'S 11.

Main Character: Con artist Danny Ocean.

What Does He Want: To rob three casinos

What's Standing In His Way: The hotel owner who stole his girl

Ticking Clock/Or Else Factor: Before they get caught.

Let's put it all together:

Con artist Danny Ocean assembles a team to rob three casinos from the hotel owner who stole his girl before they get caught.

See how easy that was?

One way to get really good at writing log lines is to practice writing them for existing novels or movies and then check your work against the official description. IMDB always contains a log line for a TV show or Movie, for example. Press releases for rights deals are another good place to find log lines of books because when Hollywood purchases a book to turn into a movie or TV show, they usually include only a single log line of the book. The New York Times Bestseller List also contains log lines.

Let's take a look at another example. This one is for THE WIZARD OF OZ.

Main Character: Dorothy, a girl stranded in a strange land

What Does She Want: To go back home.

What's Standing In Her Way: A witch that wants to kill her for revenge

When we both that all together, we get this:

After being stranded in a strange land, a girl fends off a witch that wants to kill her in order to find a way back home.

While it's technically true of the book, it's missing a lot of what makes the book special. The heart of the story is about the friendships she forms during her quest. Sometimes we need an additional element in the log line to make it really sing. We could do something like this instead:

After being stranded in a strange land, a young girl teams up with three unlikely allies in order to find a way back home before a witch kills her.

Here are a few more examples:

Log line for TITANIC:

Main Character: An aristocratic woman

What Does She Want: To escape her arranged engagement and be with the third class passenger she falls in love with

What's Standing In Her Way: Her finance

Ticking clock: The ship is sinking

An aristocratic woman falls for a third class passenger behind her fiancé's back and must find a way to be with him while trying to survive on a sinking ship.

(Yeah, yeah, she didn't quite succeed in that goal but it was still her driving force.)

Log line for PRETTY LITTLE LIARS:

Main Character: Four girls

What Do They Want: To figure out who killed their friend

What's Standing In Their Way: Someone is blackmailing them

Ticking clock: Before the blackmailer reveals their secrets

After the mysterious death of their friend, four girls must work together to find out who killed her and who is blackmailing them before the blackmailer reveals their darkest secrets.

Log line for INCEPTION:

Main Character: A team of dream architects

What Do They Want: To infiltrate a dream and plant an idea in the dreamer's mind

What's Standing In Their Way: The threat of being trapped in the dream

Ticking clock: Before the dreamer wakes

A man assembles a team to infiltrate an enemy's dream and plant an idea in his mind, but must succeed before the dreamer wakes or face being trapped in the dream forever.

EXERCISE #1:

Now you try it! Choose five different movies or TV shows and write a one sentence description of each. Then head to IMDB.com and check your work against the official description. Feel free to check my work above as well!

Chapter 3: FINDING INSPIRATION

Finding Inspiration

You know how it goes. You're in a writing slump and there seems to be no way out. You constantly feel uncreative and uninspired.

But I have a little trick to help get you back in the writing zone. I simply return to my standards for inspiration, the places that have proven time and time again to get me back into the writing groove.

Reviewing my go tos helps ground me in writing, get me into the mind-set to be able to open myself up for new ideas. When I concentrate on reviewing things that inspire me, I train my mind to be more perceptive to potential ideas. That's the goal of this technique. Not to instantly pluck ideas out of the air that weren't visible a minute ago. But to ready yourself to be able to see those ideas.

A good way to prepare yourself to find new ideas is to develop an Inspiration List. An item on the list should be in the form of a movie, a TV show, a book, or location that you constantly come back to when you need to be inspired. Coming back to the same things trains your brain to associate watching that same movie with searching for a book idea. The same way someone might use a mnemonic device to remember a difficult concept in school, EGBDF style (or as I learned in piano lessons when I was younger, Every Good Bird Does Fly, aka the black lines or notes on piano sheet music).

My inspiration mostly comes in the form of television shows. For me, it's much faster to watch an hour show for inspiration than to re-read a fave book. See? TV leads to productivity!

I'm going to share my go tos below and explain how I use them.

VOICE AND CHARACTER

I tend to write books with a lot of humor and wit in them, so I always turn to something that also has the kind of humor and wit I write. Here are my foolproof places for that:

- BUFFY THE VAMPIRE SLAYER

- VERONICA MARS

- LOST

The dialogue in Buffy and Veronica Mars automatically puts me in the mindset for witty writing. Once I'm in the mindset, funny things just fly out of my mouth (or more accurately, my fingers). I'd be really awesome at witty comebacks in real life if I was able to fuel up by watching an episode of these shows.

Veronica and Buffy also helps when I need inspiration on characters. Each character on both shows one is unique, quirky, and each side character believes they are the star of their own show even though Buffy is the protagonist. That's an important thing to remember.

Re-watching Lost helps me to dive deeper into character. I particularly like to study how the show uses flashbacks to SHOW character traits and then finds a way to twist up those traits by the end of the episode.

EMOTIONS

- My So-Called Life

- Orange is the New Black

- Grey's Anatomy

There are certain shows that just make me feel. They always put me in the teen or adult mindset and let me tap into the emotions of the characters. My So-Called Life is brilliant in the way the emotions crackle on screen until you're feeling them too.

Orange is the New Black and Grey's Anatomy are both excellent at purging tears from my eyes, getting me to emotionally connect with a variety of characters. I re-watch one of these when I want to write something that tugs at my heart strings or explores themes or subtle plot lines that explode.

PLOT

- Doctor Who

- White Collar

When I want to write something twisty, something mysterious and plot-focused, I turn to these two shows. White Collar is great for helping me identify a cool mystery that needs to be solved. Doctor Who is brilliant at showcasing a variety of sci-fi based plots that are all so very different but self contained. There are a few episodes I usually come back to, such as Blink, The Girl Who Waited, The Girl in the Fireplace.

MUSIC

Having a playlist for your writing project is not a new idea. But what about having a playlist for your writing as a whole? A few choice songs that you listen to whenever you need to get back to the writing mindset. These don't have to be about writing as a theme, but just songs you always listen to when you sit down to start writing. Here are a few of mine:

- Spirits by The Strumbellas

- Come Clean, Dark Thing by Veruca Salt

- Da Vinci by Weezer

- Motorcycle Drive By by Third Eye Blind.

- You Ruin Me by The Veronicas

- Glycerine by Bush

- High by Young Rising Sons

- Never is a Promise by Fiona Apple

- Born Again Teen by Lucius

EXERCISE #2:

Now it's your turn to create a list of a few TV shows (including specific episodes) and songs that put you back into a mindset geared toward writing or a place you need to be emotionally to connect with your genre, so you're ready to take things to the next step and start coming up with ideas. I suggest at least 5 TV shows/movies and 5 songs to get you started.

Stream Of Consciousness Inspiration List

A Stream of Consciousness Inspiration List is a great way to identify the kinds of topics that inspire you. It's a list of random things that you find interesting. You'll use this list in the next section when you start applying the various idea generation techniques to your own personal interests.

So how do you do it?

1. Turn off the Internet

2. Open up a blank document on your computer or get a pen and paper

3. Set a timer for five minutes

4. Start writing down anything you can think of that you're interested in. The key is not to stop typing/writing until the timer goes off. This can be a topic, a type of character, a

trope, a period of history, or philosophical pondering.

5. If five minutes wasn't enough, repeat the exercise.

Below you'll find a Stream of Consciousness list I created for a previous novel of mine. Several of the items in the list became plot points:

- Forbidden romances

- Bad boys that choose to turn good

- Sneaking out

- Forgotten words from English no longer in use

- Kisses that are a surprise but also inevitable, ones you wait and wait for

- Retellings of unexpected stories

- Secrets

- New technologies

- Computer programming

- Graphic design

- Art; creativity; painting

- Fonts—being able to identify them at first glance, maybe characters named after fonts

- Quoth the Raven

- School uniforms

- Chaste and forbidden sleepovers with a boy

- Secret societies

- Male best friends that are completely platonic

- Sweeping, all consuming romances

- Summer camp

- Being snowed in

- Student council elections

- Cupcakes

- Surprise twists

- Seemingly bad boy that has a secret soft side, like maybe he volunteers at a nursing home secretly

- Smart boys and even smarter girls

- Mystery

- Boy living secretly in somewhere

- History but not historical

- Playfulness

- Puns

- Unexpected settings

- Fun

- Competition (not sports)

- Hidden gems of regular towns, like an underground freestyle rap competition only a few students know about

- YouTube famous

- Speakeasies

- Beer brewing

- Heists

- Breaking the rules

- Greek Mythology

- Creepy oddities from history

- Weird facts about real towns

- Enemies to lovers

- Secret codes to crack

- Witchcraft spells that use elements, not magic

EXERCISE #3:

Now it's time to create your own list! Follow the instructions above to set a timer and free write all the things you can think of that interest you. Don't delete anything from the list after you put it down, you never know what might spark something for you in the future. Feel free to add to your list whenever you want. You can keep an ever-expanding one for all projects or create one before each new book idea you're trying to generate.

Reading For Inspiration

Sure, this one is obvious. Every writer hears the age old adage: If you want to write, you need to read, read, read!

But the difference here is in HOW you read to find inspiration. It's not reading for pleasure. It's reading for research. Reading to study. Reading to identify what makes the book you're studying work and then breaking that down into pieces you can take for yourself and re-model. I'm not talking about plagiarizing by using a similar plot or copying character traits. I'm talking about finding the very essence of the story that makes it special and understanding how the author enhanced that essence. That's the part you should emulate. Not in the same way of course but in your own way.

For example, the reason why GONE GIRL by Gillian Flynn became a bestseller sensation is because of the major, unexpected twist in the middle of the book but also because so many readers related to certain passages of the book unrelated to the twist, such as the "Cool Girl" passage. Additionally, the use of an unreliable narrator added suspense and intrigue.

That breaks down to three elements:

• An unexpected twist that turns everything upside down

• Unreliable narrator told in diary format.

• An observation on life that exploits something everyone relates to but no one discusses

From there, you can take those three elements and put your own spin on them. A different twist. A new observation about life. A narrator unreliable for a different reason and in a different way. In fact, there have been quite a few novels that came out since GONE GIRL that have taken the above elements, re-purposed them, and enjoyed their own success.

The novel THE GIRL ON THE TRAIN by Paula Hawkins contains:

• Unexpected twists that turn everything upside down. These come more as smaller but still shocking twists that make the reader question everything they know about the characters.

• Unreliable narrator. This time the structure revolves around the main characters morning and evening commute where large chunks of her day happen off the page.

• An observation on life that exploits something everyone relates to but no one discusses. These come in the form of speeches about commuting.

But that's not all.

ALL THE MISSING GIRLS by Megan Miranda contains:

- Unexpected twists that turn everything upside down. These are delivered through the unique narrative structure that's told backward.

- Unreliable narrator. As the novel goes backward in time, the reader realizes that certain scenes that already occurred take on entirely new meaning.

- An observation on life that exploits something. This comes in the form of the main character traveling back to the home town she escaped from and having a lot of feels about it, both good and bad ones.

Another example would be THE HUNGER GAMES, which paved the way for an explosion of dystopian novels.

THE HUNGER GAMES breaks down to the following key elements:

- A deadly competition (children forced to kill each other in an arena)

- A forbidden romance that seems impossible (two contestants fall in love despite the fact that only one can survive)

- A government forcing people to do something against their will

After THE HUNGER GAMES came out, several novels with similar elements followed. DIVERGENT also contains a deadly competition but in that one, more people can finish the competition alive than can in THE HUNGER GAMES. There's a forbidden romance of the instructor/student variety rather than two competitors that must kill each other. And of course, in THE HUNGER GAMES, the government forces teens into the deadly battle while in DIVERGENT, the government quite literally controls people via a simulation serum. Different executions of the same elements.

EXERCISE #4:

Break down the novel that last blew you away into three key elements that you can then re-purpose for your own needs.

Chapter 4: GENERATING IDEAS

Generating Ideas

So you've renewed your inspiration. You've written out a list of topics that interest you. You've broken down a cool novel in your chosen genre into essential elements. But how do you turn those things into ideas?

In the following sections you'll find various methods for generating ideas after you've honed in on your inspiration. Each method comes with an explanation, examples, and an exercise. Some also include pre-curated lists to help you get started. Use all the methods, use only the one that speaks to you, or use several. All of these methods have generated a book idea for me. They all work!

Research Method

Research is a great way to hone in on a specific topic that interests you and use it to generate a book idea. Research can seem daunting at first, and my method is probably the lazy man's way to research. It does not involve going to the library and poring over books on a specific topic. Google is your friend.

When I'm trying to use research to generate ideas, I go back to my Stream of Consciousness List and pick out a few topics that I'd like to dive deeper into. Here are a few from my list that I've researched, which ultimately sparked book ideas:

• Secret Societies

• Greek Mythology

• History but not historical

• Weird facts about real towns

Two of these are ones I consider easy to research—Secret Societies, Greek Mythology—while the other two are vague and therefore difficult to research. The vague kind actually provides the best ability to spark book ideas for me. But I'll discuss both types on the next few pages.

Using Research To Find Ideas

EASY RESEARCH

The reason Secret Societies and Greek Mythology falls under easy research is because both are concrete topics with a lot of information found immediately in Google. The trick is knowing where to look within that information.

SECRET SOCIETIES

When I type in "Secret Societies" these results pop up on Page 1:

• Secret society - Wikipedia, the free encyclopedia

• The 7 Most Exclusive Secret Societies in History - Huffington Post

• Top 10 Secret Societies - Listverse

• Brotherhoods and Secret Societies - Hermandades y Sociedades

• 25 Biggest Secret Societies to Ever Exist - List25

- Secret Societies Control the World - Conspiracy Theories - TIME

- How Secret Societies Stay Hidden on the Internet - The Atlantic

I find the best sites to research on are the list sites because they break down the information into bite-sized chunks. When I read the list, I'm looking for something interesting that could spawn a plot or something that can generate conflict. For example, when I read the "Top 10 Secret Societies" on Listverse, one of the entries is for "A Bilderberg Meeting." This turns out to not be a secret society in the traditional sense but an invitation-only meeting at five star hotels around the world of highly influential people to discuss secret topics. Right away I'm thinking this could be useful. How cool is that? A secret invite-only meeting. Highly influential people. Five star hotels. I might be able to work with those elements.

From there, I start mulling how this could turn into a plot. The first step is to try to determine who the Main Character might be or what the Central Conflict might be.

- Someone unexpected receives the invitation (Character)

- Invitation falls into the wrong hands (Conflict)

- Someone infiltrates the group, posing as a worker in the hotel to eavesdrop. (Character)

Once I have something that intrigues me, say it's the idea that the invitation falls into the wrong hands, I'll start to work through that further by asking questions. Who's hands? Is the wrong person the main character or an enemy? Why is it a bad thing that the invitation falls in their hands?

An alternate method is to take the information as is—invitation-only meeting at five star hotels around the world of highly influential people to discuss secret topics—and repurpose it into a new genre using those same elements.

For example, if we're going to turn this into a Sci-Fi plot, we might want to set the meeting on a space station rather than a five star hotel. Our attendees might be from other planets rather than countries. And if we use the idea above of the invitation falling into the wrong hands, the log line converts into this:

• Members of the secret meeting are from interplanetary, our hero is the representative from Earth and had no idea aliens existed until he received the invitation.

Or maybe we want to write YA and have to change the meeting into something involving teens. What happens if we set it in high school? Perhaps different members of social groups are forced together. Sounds a little BREAKFAST CLUB but we could make it work.

• In a high school with different people who seemingly have no connection thrown together via the invitations and they have to figure out who sent them and why.

Instead we might want to write a thriller so we apply key elements of thrillers to our starting information—secret meeting, hotels, discussion of secret topics. In a thriller, there's usually a bad guy. Usually the main character must figure out a way to survive and defeat the bad guy. So I start thinking of ways that could apply to our scenario. Maybe someone is killing off the members of the fictional version of the meeting. If the hero was next on the list, that would create adequate conflict.

• Someone is killing off the members of the fictional version of the meeting, one by one, and our hero is next on the list.

Each of these needs further work to become a full novel. Motivations need to be determined, mysteries intricately plotted. But we've got some bones. Once I have the above ideas, I'll cross out the ones I know are terrible or just not for me, for example, the YA version feels too low stakes compared to the others.

But don't stop there! Continue reading the other links, go deeper into the search results, and do this exercise a few times on Secret Societies to see if you can combine other interesting facts into one project. More on that later.

Chapter 5: GREEK MYTHOLOGY

I could just google Greek Mythology but that's a pretty broad topic. What I'm looking for is something interesting. So I add a keyword to my search to help me target results. When I type in "Weird Greek Mythology," the first result is "10 Things You Didn't Know About Greek Myths." I love lists that are structured like that, that present information that's supposed to shock you. Usually those lists contain gold mines. Several items on this list jump out at me but let's just focus on one:

Ares was a notorious coward whose family hates him for it, as evidenced in The Illiad.

Ares was the God of War, so I love the fact that he was a notorious coward. So very different from the way he's portrayed in mythology today. It could be interesting to write about a coward who must continually start wars.

But a character needs a plot, so from here I'll start brainstorming different scenarios for a cowardly Ares. My favorite way to brainstorm is to ask questions and then attempt to answer them.

When does the novel take place?

• During ancient times and the novel focuses on him overcoming his cowardice to become the fierce battle God remembered today.

• Takes place today. He is immortal after all.

I find the idea of the novel taking place today more interesting so I start to ponder the role a cowardly Ares had in historical wars. Maybe his cowardice is the actual cause of all the wars we've had in history. Then I try to add a ticking clock: if he doesn't stop being such a pussy...society will crumble.

Or maybe I go in a different direction entirely and I play up the fact that there's a Roman God named Mars who is the equivalent to Ares. Perhaps they have to battle each other for supremacy.

VAGUE RESEARCH

But let's say the items you want to research are of the vague kind. "History but not historical." And "Weird facts about real towns." Both of these items sparked novel ideas for me. For the first one, I perused weird history lists. I was fascinated by strange facts about history like how there's one real skull remaining at the Pirates of the Caribbean ride in Disneyland. All the skulls used to be real. *Shudders* I also came across The Underbelly Project, where anonymous artists turned an abandoned Brooklyn subway station into a graffiti showcase that no one ever sees since all entrances are sealed. Both of those turned into settings in one of my YA novels.

When you read the History section on Cracked.com, you might find lists like these:

• 23 Mad Scientists Deleted From History Books

• 6 Nightmarish Things People Did for Fun Before Electricity

- 5 First Ladies More Badass Than Their Husbands

- 21 Important Moments in History (That Were Sex-Fests)

- The 24 Creepiest Places On Earth (You Can Visit Today)

Just imagine the ideas that can spring from some of those. The creepy places might make excellent scene settings. Or maybe you get an idea to write a novel that showcases how badass one of the First Ladies was. Or maybe you're going to take your Historical Romance up to a new level with an important Sex-fest from History.

For "Weird Facts about Real Towns" I'll target different states until I find something interesting. It was this google centered around Florida that led me to learn that Ponce de Leon claimed to have found the Fountain of Youth in an area known today as St. Augustine, Florida. I wrote an entire novel based on this fact called IF EVER about the last drop of the Fountain of Youth. The novel is set in St. Augustine, Florida.

EXERCISE #5:

Choose two items from your Stream of Consciousness List, one that is easy to research and one that is vague. Google both. Read through the various links until you find something interesting. Take that interesting piece of information and jot down as many ways as you can think of to turn that interesting piece of info into a novel premise. Rinse and repeat with the next phrase. Keep the premise ideas that you might be able to work with and put them into a master list. Discard the rest.

Sites To Use For Research To Generate Ideas

• Wikipedia

• Cracked.com

• Listverse.com

• Buzzfeed.com (Science and Life sections)

- Roadtrippers.com

- Viralnova.com

- Boredomtherapy.com

- Reddit.com

- Nanowrimo.org (Forums)

- List25.com

X Meets Y

X meets Y is my favorite way to generate book ideas and perhaps the easiest since you already have log lines to work from. In Hollywood and also in the publishing industry, many projects are pitched in an "X meets Y" fashion to give the audience you are pitching to a quick way to understand the project. X meets Y simply means you're comparing your own project to elements of two well known, existing projects. You always want to use well known projects rather than obscure ones or else your clarity will be instantly lost.

The key is to use projects that boil down to a single easily identifiable premise element. It's best to choose titles where the single element would be something nearly everyone would associate with that title. For example, when people think of GROUNDHOG'S DAY, the element they recognize is a person repeating the same day over and over again. When you think of OCEAN'S 11, you think heists. When you think of TITANIC, you think ship sinking. When you think of WHEN HARRY MET SALLY, you think friends-to-lovers. If you heard ORANGE IS THE NEW BLACK as part of an X meets Y comparison, you'd automatically associate the project with prison. Same with THE STEPFORD WIVES for Robots. INCEPTION for dream stealing. THE CURIOUS CASE OF BENJAMIN BUTTON for aging backward.

Try to boil down each title to as few words as possible, preferably one or two. Prison. Robots. Aging backward. Heists. Ship sinking. Repeating same day.

The next step in the X meets Y process is to combine two elements from two different titles to create a new element. You're essentially asking the question what happens when I mix Element 1 (X) with Element 2 (Y)? What happens when you mix prison (X) with robots (Y)?

Here are some well known entities pitched in X meets Y format:

EDGE OF TOMORROW = SAVING PRIVATE RYAN meets GROUNDHOG'S DAY

- (A soldier relives the same day over and over again while trying to rescue a loved one) = (soldiers try to rescue another) + (man lives same day over and over)

HORRIBLE BOSSES = THE HANGOVER meets 9 TO 5

- (Three buddies band together to murder their bosses) = (Three buddies band together for a goal) + (Women turn the tables on their boss).

THE HUNGER GAMES = BATTLE ROYALE meets THE TRUMAN SHOW

• (Teens are forced to battle for the death on live TV) = (Teens battle to the death) + (Man's entire life is broadcast on TV)

INCEPTION = OCEAN'S 11 meets ETERNAL SUNSHINE OF THE SPOTLESS MIND

• (Team performs a heist inside someone's mind) = (Team performs a heist) + (Memories are deleted from someone's mind)

TWILIGHT = ROMEO AND JULIET meets BUFFY THE VAMPIRE SLAYER

• (Human falls in love with a vampire who wants to kill her) = (forbidden love) + (vampires)

Once you understand how the formula works, you can use it to your advantage. What I like to do is compile a huge list of potential titles that could plug into either X or Y, about 100 total. They could be a variety of genres even if I have a specific genre in mind I want to write.

You're plucking an element from the comparison, not the exact premise.

I then start picking two of the titles out of a hat at random (I actually use Excel spreadsheets and random.org to choose a row). I force myself to write out a log line of what the premise would look like for two ideas I've plucked out of the hat.

Here are some examples of X meets Ys I've picked out of a hat and the premises I came up with based on them.

INCEPTION meets FIRST WIVES CLUB

• INCEPTION = Team performs a heist inside someone's mind

• FIRST WIVES CLUB = Three divorcees seek revenge on their exes who are now dating younger women

• New Log line: A group of woman band together to invade the dreams of their ex-boyfriends' new girlfriends

THE GREAT GATSBY meets FIELD OF DREAMS

- THE GREAT GATSBY = A man becomes obsessed with an eccentric billionaire who throws lavish parties

- FIELD OF DREAMS = Voices instruct a man to build a baseball stadium for ghosts of former players

- New Log line: An eccentric rich guy is coaxed by voices to throw the most epic party ever...and the attendees are all dead.

UnREAL meets WEIRD SCIENCE

- UnREAL = Two producers resort to extreme measures to create drama on their reality show

- WEIRD SCIENCE = Two nerdy teen boys build the woman of their dreams using their computer

- New Log line: A girl working for the summer as a production assistant on a science show ends up hijacking the equipment and changing the personalities of all the cast members to meet her needs.

THE SKULLS meets MIDNIGHT IN PARIS

- THE SKULLS = A man joins an elite secret society

- MIDNIGHT IN PARIS = A man mysteriously travels to the 1920s each night and hangs out with his literary idols

- New Log line: Someone gets a weird invitation into a secret society that exists only in the past.

Some of the ideas instantly have legs to me, such as the THE SKULLS meets MIDNIGHT IN PARIS one (which I eventually outlined). Others seem harder to work with or don't interest me (UnREAL meets WEIRD SCIENCE). The key is to keep going until you find a log line premise that might work for you.

We'll delve deeper into Someone gets a weird invitation into a secret society that exists only in the past in the next section of the book.

Bonus! I've spent quite a few years curating my list of X meets Y for movies, TV shows, and some books (mostly YA). I've included my lists broken up by genre on the pages that follow, plus a quick note on the key element for each title or the log line for it. For the sake of ease, I've included Paranormal titles under Fantasy. Feel free to use my lists or create your own.

EXERCISE #6:

Put 100 titles into a hat, pick out two, and write a log line based on what you've picked out. Do this four more times until you've written five log lines.

Contemporary Titles

1. Breaking Bad

• Meth creators

2. Titanic

• Forbidden love between different classes

• Ship sinking (or doomed voyage)

3. How To Get Away With Murder

• Plotting a murder

4. Mad Men

- 60s advertising industry

5. Scandal

- Problem solvers

6. House of Cards

- Political revenge

7. Orange is the New Black

- Women's Prison

8. Rear Window

- Man observes and investigates a murder

9. Ferris Bueller

- Playing hooky

10. Dirty Dancing

- Forbidden dancing
- 60s bungalow colonies

11. Rounders

- Poker

12. Fight Club

- Anarchy

- Fighting rings

- Multiple personalities

13. First Wives Club

- Revenge on exes

14. The Royal Tenenbaums

- Prodigy children

15. The Great Gatsby

- Eccentric billionaire

- Lavish parties

16. Memento

- Murder solved backward

17. Reality Bites

- Recent college grads

18. Cruel Intentions

- Competition between step-siblings

- Elite boarding school

19. The Breakfast Club

- Motley crew trapped in the same room

20. Pretty Woman

- Prostitution

21. Camp Nowhere

- Camp without counselors

22. Dazed and Confused

- 70s teens

- Hazing

23. Eyes Wide Shut

- Sexual adventures

24. Weekend at Bernie's

- People cart around a dead person

25. Don't Tell Mom the Babysitter's Dead

• Kids left without supervision

26. Pretty Little Liars

• Blackmail via text messages

27. Downton Abbey

• Upstairs/downstairs

28. Quantico

• FBI trainees

9. Switched at Birth

• Teens discover they were switched at birth

• Deaf characters

30. Faking It

• A straight and a bisexual teen pretend to be in a F/F relationship

31. The Skulls

• Secret society

32. Romeo and Juliet

- Forbidden romance

33. Hamlet

- Family murder and revenge

34. Mistresses

- Non-traditional relationships

35. Unbreakable Kimmy Schmidt

- Cult with an upbeat tone

36. Big Bang Theory

- Science genius nerds

37. The Babysitter's Club

- Babysitting business

38. Bridesmaids

- Drama among friends of the bride

39. How I Met Your Mother

- A man tells the story of how he met his wife through a lot of unnecessary tangents and flashbacks

40. 2 Broke Girls

- Two girls come up with crazy ways to make money

41. The Bourne Identity

- A man eludes assassins while trying to regain his memory

42. Indiana Jones

- Adventure

43. Goodfellas

- Mob hierarchy

44. Pulp Fiction

- Mob hit men

- Gangster's wife

45. Friends

- A group of six in NYC

46. There's Something About Mary

- Men who vie for the same girl

47. Pride and Prejudice

- Two people must overcome their weaknesses in order to fall in love

48. Gone Girl by Gillian Flynn

- A man investigates his wife's disappearance one step ahead of the police

49. S. By JJ Abrams and Doug Dorst

- A romance plays out in the margins of a shared book

50. Girl on a Train

- A girl inserts herself into the investigation of the disappearance of a stranger

51. The Fosters

- Foster children

52. Jane the Virgin

- Telenovela-style

53. Almost Famous

- Road trip with a band

54. Devil Wears Prada

- Horrible boss in the fashion industry

55. Silver Linings Playbook

- Underdogs in a dance competition
- Struggling people connect

56. A League of Their Own

- Women's only baseball team

57. Easy A

- Scarlett Letter in high school

58. Erin Brockovich

- Underdog single handedly takes down a big company

59. American Pie

• Four teens try to lose their virginity

60. American Beauty

• A father in a mid-life crisis fantasizes about his daughter's best friend

61. Heartbreakers

• Mother/daughter con artist team

62. Coyote Ugly

• Bartenders

63. The Graduate

• Man torn between a May-December romance and a romance with her daughter

64. Clueless

• Emma with Valley Girls

65. One for the Money by Janet Evanovich

• Female bounty hunter

66. The Catch

- Woman hunts down the man that turns out to be her fiancé

67. Mr. And Mrs. Smith

- Married assassins target each other

68. Gilmore Girls

- Small town Mother/Daughter relationship

69. UnREAL

- Two producers resort to extreme measures to create drama on their reality show

70. Veronica Mars

- Teen solves crimes

71. Gossip Girl

- Wealthy popular kids in New York City

72. Grey's Anatomy

- Social lives of surgeons

73. Criminal Minds

- Analyzing the minds of criminals

74. Glee

- School glee club made of diverse members

75. New Girl

- Roommates

Romance Titles

1. Crazy Ex-Girlfriend

- A woman follows her childhood crush across the country

2. How to Lose a Guy in 10 Days

- Rival magazine editors use each other for story material

3. The Intern

- A widower takes an internship post-retirement

4. Bride Wars

- Two brides engage in rivalry

5. Hitch

- A professional date doctor

6. When Harry Met Sally

- Friends-to-lovers

7. Romeo and Juliet

- Forbidden romance

8. Since You've Been Gone

- Quirky scavenger hunt

9. You've Got Mail

- Rival business owners fall in love anonymously online

10. Sleepless in Seattle

- A man and woman fall in love via a radio call-in show

11. 27 Dresses

- Always a bridesmaid, never a bride

12. Failure to Launch

- A grown man refuses to leave his parents' house

13. Couples Retreat

- Couples are forced into therapy at a resort

14. 500 Days of Summer

- Non-linear hipster romance

15. Nick and Norah's Infinite Playlist

- Romantic hijinks in one night around New York City

16. Forgetting Sarah Marshall

- A man takes a vacation to forget his ex at the same resort she's vacationing at too

17. Knocked Up

- A pregnancy results from a one-night stand

18. Music and Lyrics

- A man and woman fall in love while writing a song

19. Notting Hill

• An A-list celebrity falls for a commoner

20. The Holiday

• Love among AirBNB

21. Wedding Crashers

• Men fall for women at a wedding they crash

22. Fever Pitch

• A woman falls for a guy who loves baseball a little too much

23. The 40-Year-Old Virgin

• Delayed virginity loss

24. 50 First Dates

• A man falls for a woman with amnesia

25. Love Actually

• Vignettes about love (and sometimes heartbreak)

26. My Big Fat Greek Wedding

- Big family

27. She's All That

- A bet to turn a girl hot by prom that seems impossible except all they need to do is remove her glasses and ponytail

28. Never Been Kissed

- A journalist poses as a high school student and falls for her teacher

29. The Wedding Singer

- A wedding singer falls for a caterer

30. My Best Friend's Wedding

- A woman tries to stop her best friend's wedding so he'll fall for her instead

31. While You Were Sleeping

- A woman pretends to be engaged to an unconscious man

32. The Cutting Edge

- Figure skating partners fall in love

33. Four Weddings and a Funeral

- A committed bachelor falls in love over the course of four social events

34. Overboard

- A man pretends a girl with amnesia is his wife

35. Working Girl

- A secretary pretends to be the boss

36. Pretty in Pink

- A girl torn between her childhood sweetheart and a playboy

37. High Fidelity

- A man tracks down his exes to learn why he's a sucky boyfriend

38. The Proposal

- Sham marriage

39. Going the Distance

- Long distance relationship

40. Shakespeare in Love

- Love between a playwright and his muse

41. Two Weeks Notice

- A woman walks out on her boss

42. HouseSitter

- A con artist moves into a man's house and poses as his wife against his knowledge

43. Friends with Benefits

- Two colleagues add sex to their friendship

44. The Fault in our Stars by John Green

- Love among two terminally ill teens

45. 50 Shades of Grey by E. L. James

- Billionaire S&M

46. Perfect Chemistry by Simone Elkeles

- Love between two people on different sides of the tracks

47. Twilight by Stephenie Meyer

• Forbidden romance with a vampire

48. Me Before You by JoJo Moyes

• A woman falls for the quadriplegic man she's charged with caring for

49. The Notebook by Nicholas Sparks

• A poor man falls for a rich woman

50. Sixteen Candles

• A girl has a terrible sixteenth birthday (except for the part about Jake)

Science Fiction Titles

1. Stepford Wives

• Robots

2. Contact

• Science vs Religion after aliens make contact

3. Jurassic Park

• Dinosaurs in an amusement park

4. Inception

• Dream heists

5. Gattaca

• Gene manipulation

6. Weird Science

• Teens create the woman of their dreams in their computer

7. Secret World of Alex Mack

• Girl receives special powers after getting spilled on with experimental material

8. Defending your Life

• Man must justify his life in purgatory

9. Doctor Who episode: THE GIRL WHO WAITED

• People trapped in different time streams

10. Doctor Who episode: THE GIRL IN THE FIREPLACE

- Lovers keep disconnecting across time

11. Doctor Who episode: BLINK

- People trapped in the past need to be rescued by someone in the future

12. Mr. Robot

- Trippy techno-thriller with multiple personalities
- Hackers

13. Orphan Black

- Clones

14. Gravity

- Woman trapped in space

15. The Martian

- Man trapped on Mars

16. Jessica Jones

- Superhero becomes investigator

17. Dark Matter

- People on a space ship with amnesia must figure out if they're the good guys or not

18. Firefly

- Space opera

19. Star Wars

- Battles in space using the force

20. The Matrix

- A hacker battles in cyberspace

21. Eternal Sunshine of the Spotless Mind

- Erasing memories

22. Back to the Future

- A man is trapped in the past

23. Quantum Leap

- A man can jump into other people's bodies

24. Edge of Tomorrow

- A soldier fighting aliens relives the same day over and over again

25. Interstellar

• Time speeds as a man travels through a wormhole in space

26. Ex-machina

• A man evaluates a human like A.I.

27. Minority Report

• A man is accused of a crime he'll commit in the future

28. Snowpiercer

• A group of survivors in a frozen apocalypse travel through the class system-based cars of a train

29. The Host

• Aliens inhabit people's bodies

30. District 9

• A government agent helps a quarantined extraterrestrial race

31. Her

- A man falls in love with an Operating System

32. Another Earth

- Another earth is discovered in a different solar system

33. Sliders

- A group of people travel to parallel universes

34. Looper

- A man is sent to the past to be murdered

35. The 100

- Delinquent teens are sent to a post-apocalyptic Earth

36. Legends of Tomorrow

- A group of superheroes hunt a villain across time

37. Doctor Who

- A man travels through time and space to help people

38. Source Code

- A man inhabits someone else's body to stop a bomber on a train

39. Killjoys

- Space bounty hunters

40. Battlestar Galactica

- A crew protects a small colony on their way to Earth

41. Uglies by Scott Westerfeld

- A world where plastic surgery is mandatory

42. Delirium by Lauren Oliver

- A world where love is considered a disease and has been cured

43. A Wrinkle in Time by Madeleine L'Engle

- Three kids travel in time and space

44. Across the Universe by Beth Revis

- Two teens solve a murder aboard a generation ship bound for a new planet

45. These Broken Stars by Megan Spooner and Amie Kaufman

- Two teens are stranded on an uninhabited planet...so they think

46. Illuminae by Amie Kaufman and Jay Kristoff

- A spaceship operating system becomes self aware and tries to murder everyone on board

47. Cinder by Marissa Meyer

- Cinderella with Cyborgs

48. The 5th Wave by Rick Yancey

- Aliens have taken over humanity, this time by inhabiting them

49. A Thousand Pieces of You by Claudia Gray

- A girl hunts a villain through parallel worlds

50. Edward Scissorhands

- A gentle monster whose creator died before he could give him hands

51. Extant

- A woman travels to space alone and comes back pregnant

52. Lost

- A plane crashes on a mysterious island

53. Dollhouse

- Personalities can be infused into people

54. The Time Traveler's Wife

- A man with a gene that causes him to involuntarily travel through time

55. Resurrection

- Dead people mysteriously come alive decades later

56. Revolution

- A world without wifi (or other electronics)

Fantasy Titles

1. The Odyssey

- A man encounters fantastical obstacles on his journey home to his wife

2. Sleepy Hollow

- Man hunts headless horseman

3. Red Queen by Victoria Aveyard

- The color of a person's blood grants super powers

4. Macbeth

- A man and his scheming wife seize the throne

5. Gulliver's Travels

- A man encounters strange lands during his travels

6. A Darker Shade of Magic by V.E. Schwab

- A man possesses the ability to travel to alternate versions of London

7. Vicious by V.E. Schwab

- Origin story of two villains

8. Game of Thrones

- Battle for a throne

9. Peter Pan

- A land where kids never age; pirates

10. Alice's Adventures in Wonderland

- A girl falls through a rabbit hole into a strange land

11. Wizard of Oz

- After being stranded in a strange land, a young girl teams up with three unlikely allies in order to find a way back home before a witch kills her.

12. Scott Pilgrim vs the World

- A man must defeat the exes of his new girlfriend

13. Throne of Glass by Sarah J Maass

- A competition for assassins

14. The Princess Bride

- A man battles to save the woman he loves from a marriage she doesn't want

15. The Shannara Chronicles

- Two elves travel to restore the magic to a protective tree

16. Lord of the Rings

- Companions set out to destroy a powerful ring

17. Pan's Labyrinth

- A girl escapes into an eerie land

18. Harry Potter

- A school for magic

19. The Magicians

- A grad school for magic

20. The Never-Ending Story

- A boy enters a fantasy world through the pages of a book

21. Pirates of the Caribbean

- A man teams up with a pirate to save his love from undead pirates

22. Beauty and the Beast

- A girl falls for a man cursed to be a beast

23. The Walking Dead

- Zombies

24. The Little Mermaid

- A mermaid trades her voice for legs

25. Cinderella

- A fairy godmother grants a maid an unforgettable night at a ball

26. Rapunzel

- A woman locked in a tower is saved thanks to her long hair

27. Snow White and the Seven Dwarfs

- A woman's step mother hires a hit man to kill her but he falls for her instead

28. Jumanji

- A board game comes alive

29. Hercules/Xena

- Mythological battles

30. The Witches

- A boy stumbles on a witch convention

31. The Craft

- Four teens start a coven

32. Outlander by Diana Gabaldon

- A woman is swept back in time

33. Aladdin

- A thief finds a genie lamp and gets three wishes

34. Beetlejuice

- Two ghosts try to rid their house of humans

35. Island of Dr. Moreau

- An island with a mad scientist who turns animals into experimental humans

36. Teen Wolf

- Teens battling werewolves and other supernatural creatures

37. Vampire Diaries

- Small town vampire romance

38. Buffy the Vampire Slayer

- Slayer fights off vampires and other demons

39. Once Upon a Time

- Fairy tale characters have no recollection of their past

40. Charmed

- A family of witches

41. Agents of Shield

- Secret agents battle the supernatural

42. American Horror Story

- Anthology series that centers on different creepy themes

43. Lost Girl

- Succubus

44. Lucifer

- The devil quits Hell and helps solve crimes in LA

45. Being Human

- A ghost, vampire, and werewolf share a house

46. Ghostbusters

- A team of four battles ghosts

47. Graceling by Kristin Cashore

- A girl is graced with the gift of killing

48. The Hunger Games by Suzanne Collins

• Teens are forced to battle to the death on live TV

49. The Girl from Everywhere by Heidi Hellig

• A girl uses ancient maps to travel to the places depicted on the maps

50. The Snow Queen

• An evil queen who unleashes a frozen tundra on the world

Magical Realism Titles

1. Big

• A child's wish to be grown is granted overnight

2. Being John Malkovich

• People take control of someone else's mind

3. Amelie

• Random acts of kindness

4. Midnight in Paris

- A man mysteriously travels to the 1920s each night and hangs out with his literary idols

5. Groundhog's Day

- A man relives the same day over and over

6. Field of Dreams

- Voices instruct a man to build a baseball stadium for ghosts of former players

7. Pleasantville

- Two teens are transported into the world of a TV show

8. Night at the Museum

- Figures at a museum come alive

9. Death Becomes Her

- Two rivals cheat death and then engage in an epic battle for supremacy

10. We Were Liars by E. Lockhart

- Teen struggles to recall an event that happened in her past

11. Peggy Sue Got Married

- Teen transported back into her own past to correct her mistakes

12. Good Luck Chuck

- Man must break curse that enables women to fall in love with someone else after sleeping with him

13. Like Water for Chocolate

- A woman infuses her emotions into her food

14. Donnie Darko

- Man receives clues about the world ending from a giant bunny

15. The Green Mile

- A man on death row possesses a mysterious gift

16. Prelude to a Kiss/Vice Versa/Freaky Friday

- Two people accidentally switch bodies

17. The Legend of Bagger Vance

- A golfer recovers his game with the help from a mysterious caddy

18. It's a Wonderful Life

- A man is shown what the world would be like without him in it

19. Practical Magic

- Witches use their gift for magic to overcome obstacles in love

20. The Raven Boys series by Maggie Stiefvater

- A magical forest that produces dream objects, a quest for a sleeping king that can grant witches, and a whole lot of weirdness exists in a small town

21. Landline by Rainbow Rowell

- A woman speaks to her husband in the past

22. Down with the Shine by Kate Karyus Quinn

• A girl grants wishes with moonshine

23. The Curious Case of Benjamin Button

• A man ages backward

24. Pushing Daises

• Man kills anyone he touches

25. The Age of Adaline

• A woman never ages

26. 13 Going on 30

• A 13-year-old girl's wish to be 30 is granted

27. What Women Want

• A man can hear what women are thinking

28. The Night Circus by Erin Morgenstern

• A magical circus that only opens at night

29. Mary Poppins

- A magical nanny

30. The Lake House

- A man and a woman from different years communicate via letters placed in the same mailbox

31. When in Rome

- An unlucky woman tosses a coin into a fountain and must fend off suitors

32. Sliding Doors

- A story of two different outcomes from the same decision, told in parallel

33. Click

- A remote allows a man to fast forward or rewind his life

Using Plot Formulas

Some of the most established writers utilize formulas in their writing to great effect. Formulas help give the writers an instant plot because the structure is already laid out and the writer just needs to fill in the details. The variables change to make each story unique but the essential, overarching plot is generally the same. To better illustrate what I mean, I've listed a few examples below:

Formulas in John Green books:

• Protagonist is usually quiet and naive

• There is always a witty, diverse sidekick

• The main character always falls for some form of Manic Pixie Dream Girl (or boy!)

• The main character is always obsessed with something quirky that translates into the plot. (Famous last words for Looking for Alaska, Rene Magritte painting for The Fault in our Stars, etc)

• Example for LOOKING FOR ALASKA: Quiet, naive Miles befriends The Colonel, a strategic mastermind behind pranks, and Takumi Hikohito, a hip-hop enthusiast, at his new boarding school. He falls for enigmatic Alaska Young, who turns Miles's life upside down.

- Example for PAPER TOWNS: Shy, naive Quentin embarks on a scavenger hunt with his best friend Radar, a guy whose family owns the world's largest collection of black Santa figurines, in order to find the love of Quentin's life Margo who disappeared and left behind quirky clues to her whereabouts.

Formulas in Sarah Dessen books:

- Main character usually has a dead or absent parent

- Main character usually has a flaw or hang up that directly opposes the way of life of the boy she meets

- She usually has a fierce group of friends, either existing ones or brand new.

- There is usually a quirky subplot

- Example for THE TRUTH ABOUT FOREVER: After her father dies unexpectedly, Macy requires stability and perfection to keep her life in order, but she meets a boy who works at a chaotic catering business where nothing goes as planned. She becomes fast friends with the girls from the catering company. Strange products keep arriving at her house.

• Example for SAINT ANYTHING: After her brother gets incarcerated, Sydney's parents throw all their focus on him, making her disappear in her own home. But she meets Mac, a watchful boy who really sees her for the first time. His sister Layla searches for the perfect fry dipping sauce.

Formulas in Richelle Mead books

• Most of Richelle's books involve a kidnapping of some kind during the book's climax

• There's usually a forbidden romance

• A major cliff hanger in book 3 of a series

• Due to spoilers, I won't give examples, but trust me on this!

Stepping back further, a popular Hollywood notion is that every story contains three important characters:

- Protagonist: Someone who wants something specific and tangible that can be achieved over the course of the story

- Antagonist: Someone stopping the Protagonist from getting what they want

- Relationship character: Someone the Protagonist leans on for wisdom or support. Note: the relationship character does not need to be a romantic one.

A specific, tangible goal means something that is quantifiable, not vague. A character who wants freedom is not specific. A character who wants freedom by escaping from jail/a stifling town/a bad relationship is specific and tangible.

Romantic comedies generally follow this simple formula:

- Boy meets girl

- Boy loses girl

- Boy gets girl back

But some stories twist upon the usual romantic comedy formula.

- Boy meet girl...because she's stalking him: GIRL ON A TRAIN

- Boy meets girl...at a support group for terminally ill patients: THE FAULT IN OUR STARS

- Boy loses girl...because he ages backward: THE CURIOUS CASE OF BENJAMIN BUTTON

- Boy loses girl in the first few minutes of the movie: BACK TO THE FUTURE

Horror genres contain their own tried and true formulas such as a group is stalked and has no place to hide. Formulas are universal. They are used over and over for a reason: because they make for good stories as long as you make the variables unique.

Formulas can also come in the form of the same plot that's told in different ways in different versions. How many stories have you read in which someone goes on a quest?

LORD OF THE RINGS centers on a quest to destroy the ring. STAR WARS follows Luke's quest to defeat Darth Vader.

The best way to use formulas to generate ideas is to take a formula and ask questions about it until you can expand it into something usual. For example, let's take one of the formulas listed above:

A group is stalked by a killer and has no place to hide.

We start by asking the obvious questions: who/what, where, why.

• What kind of group? Where are they located that they have no place to hide? Why is the killer targeting them?

Some potential answers:

1) Strangers (who) on a plane (where) targeted due to proximity (why)

2) Friends (who) at a house party (where) targeted due to revenge (why)

3) Teammates on a soccer team (who) targeted before an away game due (where) to rivalry (why)

Once we have some basic information, we can turn those into log lines:

1) Passengers on a twelve-hour flight over the ocean must band together to survive as a killer takes them out, one by one.

2) A house party turns deadly when one attendee seeks revenge on everyone else.

3) Soccer rivalry explodes when the home team stalks the rival team to the death.

To get you started, I've included a list of several different basic formulas you can use to get started. Turn to the next page to read them.

EXERCISE #7:

Take one of the formulas listed above or on the next page and twist the variables to make it your own. Ask different questions about the formula to help expand it.

List Of Tried And True Formulas

1. Boy meets girl, Boy loses girl, Boy gets girl back

2. Girl meets boy whose strength balances out her biggest flaw

3. Boy meets Manic Pixie Dream Girl

4. Forbidden romance

5. A group is stalked by a killer and has no place to hide

6. The villain gets caught on purpose

7. Hero goes under cover to infiltrate the bad guys

8. Someone close to the protagonist is murdered

9. Someone is being blackmailed

10. Someone new comes to town

11. Someone from the past comes back to town

12. Someone takes a trip

13. Someone goes on a quest

14. Man tries to save the world

15. Rags to riches

16. An unnatural event occurs

17. A natural disaster occurs

18. Someone enters a competition

19. Someone seeks revenge

20. Someone seeks redemption

Using Tropes - Part 1

Tropes, by definition, are a common theme or device. On their own, they can be cliche. But when combined or subverted, they can be used to help generate ideas. A subverted trope is simply a trope turned upside down somehow. Each genre has its own trope conventions. For example, in Romance, there's the enemies to lovers trope, return to hometown, best friend's brother, stranded together. In Horror, phones might be dead, someone might be trapped somewhere as the killer approaches, it might be storming outside, it's always night.

Combining two or more of these tropes can often generate an instant plot.

Let's take the romance tropes listed above and combine them into one plot. We've got a guy who returns to his hometown where he encounters his little sister's best friend who he hates for some reason. Somehow they get stranded together and find love as a result. Okay, that's a start but sounds a little generic, let's add some details by asking questions. What kind of guy is he now? What does he do for a living? Why does he return to his hometown? Why does he hate his best friends little sister? How and where do they get stranded together?

Then we start to answer those questions by plugging in a few different options. First, I list out a bunch of options for each question.

What kind of guy is he now?

- A bad boy

- A nice guy

- A nerd

- A hipster

- A hard-worker

What does he do for a living?

- An entrepreneur

- A lawyer

- A soldier

- A scientist

- A con artist

Why does he return to his hometown?

- For a funeral

- He returns from war

- For a business deal

- To perform a heist

- For a convention

Why does he hate his best friends little sister?

- She turned him down stone cold in high school

- They used to be epic rivals or are current rivals

- She got him fired from a job or expelled from school

- She got rich, he didn't

- She got the job he wanted

How and where do they get stranded together?

- A car they're riding in breaks down in the middle of nowhere

- There's a blackout someplace and both are them are inside

- One of them is in danger and they go into hiding

- They get trapped inside a building

- They get arrested together and thrown in the same jail cell

Now take some of your answers and combine them into log lines.

An entrepreneur returns home to secure a lucrative business deal with a hot new company…that's run by his former rival from high school who also happens to be his best friend's little sister. As he tries to woo her for his company with a big, extravagant trip, they get stranded on the way.

A military soldier returns home from deployment where he runs into his little sister's best friend, aka the girl who broke his heart when she turned him down stone cold all those years ago. But when a local crime puts her in danger, he uses his combat training to try to rescue her—even if it means getting trapped himself.

A con artist returns to his home town to pull his biggest job to date—a heist on the richest girl in town aka his little sister's best friend. If he succeeds in stealing her expensive diamond ring, he'll earn both the cash he needs to pay off his debts and the revenge he's been seeking on her ever since she got him expelled from high school ten years ago.

The above plots need work for sure, but this should give you an idea of how to take tropes and combine them to give you different options. On the next page, I've listed out common Romance tropes to get you started. Romance tropes can be used to generate plots in other genres since all novels center on a relationship of some kind, whether romantic or not. Start with choosing a few tropes and then twist them into the genre you want to write in.

EXERCISE #8:

Choose two or three tropes from the next page and use them to create three different plot ideas by plugging in different variables.

List Of Romance Tropes

Please note, almost all of these could work for same sex relationships as well.

1. Friends to lovers

- The hero and heroine start as friends but fall in love over the course of the book. Maybe it's a platonic roommate that turns not so platonic. Or a friend from high school that's always there for the protagonist. Or a work colleague that becomes a partner in the bedroom as well.

2. Enemies to lovers

- The hero and heroine hate each other and that hatred sparks romance. Maybe they're competing against each other for something. Or they're business rivals. Or their personalities clash.

3. Step-sibling romance

- blood but by marriage and their attraction grows.

4. Brother's best friend or Best friend's brother

- The heroine falls for the one guy she can't have: her brother's best friend. This can be gender-swapped as well.

5. Boy next door

- The main character falls for the person she's known her whole life, the one who has always lived right near her.

6. Second chance romance

- The lovers were in a previous relationship that didn't last. Now they have another chance to make it work.

7. Secret baby

- She's pregnant and hasn't told him yet. Or he has a baby with another woman and hasn't told her.

8. Sudden baby

- One or both of them inherit someone else's child unexpectedly. Or a child the man didn't know about shows up out of the blue.

9. Accidental pregnancy

- She gets pregnant by accident, often as a result of a one night stand with the hero.

10. Marriage of convenience

- The hero and heroine need to get married to prevent some kind of conflict, such as one of them being deported or to avoid an arranged marriage.

11. Arranged marriage

- The hero and heroine are forced into a marriage. Sometimes this is the result of a culture or society. Sometimes it's the result of the government (generally in fantasy or dystopian).

12. Fake relationship

- The hero and heroine pretend to be in a relationship to fool someone else. Maybe they need domestic partner health insurance. Maybe they are trying to sneak into an event by pretending to be a couple.

13. Billionaire

- He's a sexy billionaire with a penchant for expensive suits and sometimes bondage.

14. Alpha male

- He's strong, driven, and completely in control. And probably depicted on the cover shirtless.

15. Bad boy or Bad boy turns good

- He's sexy because he doesn't follow the rules. He likely has tattoos. He's done something bad that is likely forgivable. Sometimes he turns from an all out asshole into a guy worthy of the heroine's affections (Spike from Buffy the Vampire Slayer for example) .

16. Rocker (with tattoos)

- He's the lead singer or guitarist in a band and likely has the requisite tattoos.

17. Soldier

- He fought hard in the war and now he's going to fight hard for her heart.

18. Cowboy

• He rides a horse and wears a cowboy hat—except when he's naked. Okay maybe sometimes when he's naked.

19. Player

• This guy is hard to tame but the heroine's going to be the one to do it.

20. No strings attached

• It's a casual fling. Nothing more. They don't have feelings for each other. Nope. Wait… Maybe. Okay, yes, they do. Crap, they fell in love.

21. Friends with benefits

• This is slightly different from No Strings Attached in that a solid friendship precedes the sexual relationship whereas a friendship is not a requisite for a no strings attached relationship.

22. One night stand

- It was only supposed to be one night but because this is a romance novel, it's going to be more. A lot more. Happily ever after's worth of more.

23. Mistaken identity

- One of them is mistaken by the other for someone they are not. They'll probably be pissed when they learn the truth but they're going to get over it.

24. Road trip

- The two embark on a road trip together. There will likely be a hotel that only has a single bed they have to share.

25. Stranded together

- The two are stranded somewhere unexpectedly. Maybe their boat gets stuck at sea during a storm. Or their car breaks down. Or they're in a dystopian maze and can't find their way out.

26. Forced to work together

- The two are placed together on a project they can't get out of. Maybe it's a work assignment. Maybe it's a school project. Maybe it's community service.

27. On the rocks

- The two are already in a relationship that isn't going very well. Over the course of the book, they have to save it.

28. On the run

- The hero and heroine are fleeing from something. Maybe that something is dangerous in the from of a villain. Maybe it's dangerous in the form of a tornado. Maybe it's dangerous in the form of a shady business deal.

29. Return to hometown

- Either the hero or heroine returns to their hometown after many years away while the other one has never left. Maybe they both return home at the same time.

30. In peril

- The hero or heroine is in danger and only the other can save them. This could be called damsel in distress but who says it's the woman who needs rescuing?

31. Epic crush

- One pines for the other while the other either has no idea or doesn't return those feelings (yet, obviously).

32. Virgin

- Either the hero or heroine has never had sex. But (s)he's about to!

33. Guardian

- The hero takes the heroine under his protection. Maybe it's in the form of a bodyguard situation. Or someone assigned by law to watch over the other.

34. Instructor/Student

- One of the two is a teacher of some sort, maybe a professor at a college, a T.A., maybe at a yoga class the other takes at the gym. The other is the instructor's student. They're not supposed to get together. It's totally wrong to date your instructor, especially your yoga instructor.

35. Work colleagues

• Office romance, usually the forbidden kind where they work for a not-so-progressive company and had to sign a contract forbidding all office relations. Yay conflict! In the work colleague scenario, they are on equal job levels.

36. Boss/subordinate

• This is similar to office romance except a clause is not necessary but there's definitely a stigma to dating your boss. Even when he's so sexy in those suits. And when he takes control of a meeting. And when he offers you that raise that may or may not be a result of sleeping with him (spoiler alert, it's not).

37. May/December

- One of the two is significantly younger than the other.

38. Disguise

- One of the two is in disguise or undercover and fools the other into thinking they are someone they're not. Maybe one is an undercover cop. Maybe she's a con artist pulling a long con. Maybe he's in the witness protection program. Maybe it's a maid disguising herself as a princess.

39. Different social classes

- This is a popular Historical trope in which a lady of stature falls for one of the help. Or a prince falls for a commoner. Society frowns upon these kind of matches, but I suspect readers won't!

Title Generated Ideas

Generating an idea from a title is when you come up with the title first and then figure out a premise to go with it. Cool titles can be found all over the place. Song titles can't be copy righted like lyrics so they're the perfect place to start. Another great place to find titles is episode titles from favorite TV shows. Or look up puns. Punny titles can work great in the right genre. PREMATURE EVACUATION (book 1 in my NA romance series) is a pun-based title and one of the things that sparked the book idea. Or choose a cool turn of phrase you heard somewhere or read in a book. There is also a forum on nanowrimo.com where people leave cool sounding titles for other users to "adopt."

You want to choose a title that sparks an instant premise. Not something vague and pithy. Don't get me wrong, pithy titles can work great on a final product, but they are often difficult to generate ideas from.

Please note, even if you use the song title to generate a book idea, that doesn't mean you have to use that title as the final one for your own novel. This could just be a jumping off point.

So how do you go from title to a book idea? Let's go through the motions.

We'll start with a song title. Something recognizable and catchy. Taylor Swift titles often make for great romance boo premises. For the purposes of this demonstration, we're going to use Shake It Off.

The song itself is in reference to Taylor shaking off all the negative things the media says about her. But I start by thinking of all the potential plots that could work with that title. Shake it off can mean quite a few things:

• Urban Dictionary defines the phrase in four ways: To forget about someone or something. To let go. To get over it. To move on.

• The Free Dictionary says this could be a reference to the phrase give someone the shake in reference to out running someone who is following you. The attackers were in pursuit but we gave them the shake.

• There are literal definitions: to dislodge something by shaking: we shook off the dirt from the blanket.

• It can also mean to get back up and keep trying.

• We can be punny with it. Maybe the word Shake in this case is in reference to a Milkshake.

• Or we could try to think of other things that shake.Maracas. Pom poms.

Let's take each one of these and try to think of plot options that fit them. The way I come up with these is mulling scenarios in which the phrase would become true.

To forget about someone or something. To let go. To get over it. To move on.

• A girl shaking off a past relationship by searching for a new one.

- A girl shaking off a past hardship by moving to a new city and starting fresh.

Chapter 6: Give someone the shake

- A criminal on the run from the law must continually find ways to give them the shake.

- A woman being stalked by a serial killer and must try to outsmart her attacker.

To dislodge something by shaking

- A spaceship with an enemy ship lodged onto it like plankton clinging to a whale. The spaceship has to find a way to shake it off and free itself.

- A man possessed by a spirit he must rid from his body.

Get back up and keep trying

- Someone injured by something (like thrown off a horse) must get back on that horse to win a race.

- Someone fired from a job that now has to restart her whole career.

Pun-based title

- A woman leaves her big corporate job to follow her dream of purchasing a food truck and selling artisinal milkshakes.

Literal shaking

- A story about people trapped after an epic earthquake

- A novel about cheerleaders who shake their pom poms.

Already that's a lot of ideas. Some are clearly better than others. I'm going to choose three to dive deeper into and try to tease out a more concrete book idea. I'm going to specifically choose a mixture of vague and concrete ideas to play with each. Here are the three we're going to work with:

- A girl shaking off a past hardship by moving to a new city and starting fresh.

- A woman leaves her big corporate job to follow her dream of purchasing a food truck and selling artisinal milkshakes.

- A novel about cheerleaders who shake their pom poms.

A girl shaking off a past hardship by moving to a new city and starting fresh.

This one is clearly vague with not a lot of plot and conflict. Let's try to find some by asking questions. What is the past hardship she needs to shake off? Why does she move to a new city? What city exactly—does it have any relevance to the plot? What does starting fresh mean for HER?

And then I try to answer those questions with a few ideas for each in quick stream of consciousness sprint format.

What is the past hardship she needs to shake off?

- A death in the family

- Being fired

- Town gossip running rampant about her

For the next set of questions, I try to answer in line with the answers I already have to see if I can build a plot.

Why does she move to a new city and which city does she move to?

• She inherited an estate belonging to the dead relative and either has to clean it out or make it her new residence. It resides in a quirky seaside town that's very different from her big city life.

• She didn't like her old job anyway so she moves to Hollywood to pursue her dream of acting.

• The gossip in her small town linked her to a crime she didn't commit but is accused of or maybe the gossip was in relation to a close relative (spouse?) who committed a crime and now she wants to distance herself from the judging eyes. She moves to a large city where she can disappear in a crowd.

From there I eliminate the ones that aren't working. The Hollywood story doesn't interest me as much as the others, so I nix it. But there may be something there with inheriting an estate someone needs to clean up. I start to figure out what the conflict might be. What secrets could she uncover while cleaning out the house? Maybe there's a mystery she uncovers via the items—a diary? Something stolen? A dead body buried under the floor boards?—and sets out to solve it. Is anyone in the new town eager to acquire some of the items inside the estate, maybe because they don't want anyone else finding them or maybe just in a competition sort of way? What sort of people might she meet in the new town?

Or the gossip one. I'm intrigued by the idea that a woman leaves her spouse and her small town life behind after her husband is accused of a crime she can't stomach being connected to. She can't look her husband in the eye and chooses to abandon him rather than face him. Maybe he murdered someone. Maybe he's a teacher and had an affair with a student. So she sets out to an anonymous new place, a big city. But she'd obviously need to encounter conflict. Maybe someone from her old town moves there too. Maybe detectives try to find her and the reader learns she's an unreliable narrator and is connected to the crime in a surprising way.

I keep asking questions, digging deeper, trying to find the right conflict until I have the seeds of a story that demands to be written.

The same process would work for a pun-based title, like how I came up with PREMATURE EVACUATION. What would be evacuated prematurely? A relationship! And I kept going from there. Maybe the guy is allergic to commitment. Etc.

EXERCISE #10:

Select one song title or a cool turn of phrase and try to work through it to figure out what stories might be told about that topic. Remember, it's okay to take the story in a direction where the original title no longer fits. The purpose is to use the title as a jumping off point.

Twisting Existing Ideas

Twisting existing ideas is a great way to generate your own book ideas. This method has been done countless times in the past. Every time Hollywood reboots a franchise, they are twisting an existing idea into a new one. Every time someone writes a retelling or reimagining of a classic story, they are twisting an existing idea.

So how do you do it? How do you take something that isn't yours and change it enough to make it your own? The key is that you have to change enough of it so it no longer resembles the original idea you borrowed from. Or if it does resemble it, it's in an intentional retelling based way. But be careful of legal ramifications. Retellings of works in the Public Domain are fair game. Anything else will require copyright permission.

There are three ways to twist an existing idea:

1. Write a retelling

- In this scenario, you take a classic story and find a way to spin it into something new.

2. Another POV

- In this scenario, you take a classic story but tell it from another POV.

3. Rewriting a blurb

- In this scenario, you take any story (in Public Domain or not) and change some of the variables in the blurb until it becomes something new.

On the pages that follow, I'll walk you through how to generate ideas using each technique.

HOW TO CREATE A RETELLING

In the steps below, I'll walk you through exactly how to create a retelling.

1. Make a list of four classic stories you might want to reimagine.

Classic stories MUST be in the Public Domain. A story in the Public Domain is free to use legally for commercial projects. There is no fear of copyright infringement. Any stories not in the public domain are subject to permission fees. A story enters the public domain seventy years after the author's death. All the classic stories you know and love are likely in the Public Domain. Shakespeare. Poe. Jane Austen. Lewis Carroll.

When choosing the four stories you might want to imagine, ignore genre. If it's historical, it can be made contemporary. If it's fantasy, it can be retold without magical elements. If it's a classic love story set in our world, it can be re-set in a fantasy or sci-fi world.

Choose stories with a clear main character that contains traits and a character arc you might want to write about. Elizabeth Bennett possesses a fierce prejudice she must overcome. Alice is filled with curiosity and whimsy. Peter Pan is youthful and carefree but also kills lost boys in the original story.

Example:

- ALICE IN WONDERLAND

- PETER PAN

- PRIDE AND PREJUDICE

- THE WIZARD OF OZ

2. Write out the central plot of each in log line format.

- Alice follows a mysterious rabbit to a strange, new world and experiences crazy adventures as she seeks for a way into the beautiful garden.

- Wendy and her brothers follow a flying boy to a new land where kids do not age and battle with Pirates. She accepts the role of their mother and must decide whether she wants to stay or leave and grow up.

- Elizabeth Bennett and Mr. Darcy come from different classes and both overcome their biggest weaknesses—hers prejudice, his pride—to fall in love with each other in a society that would otherwise frown on their union.

• A girl stranded in a strange land bands with a group of outcasts who each want something different. They work together to achieve their goals, even if it means fending off a witch and finding an elusive wizard.

3. Change a few words in your plot description to twist a few elements in order to make it your own. This could mean changing genre, swapping genders, etc.

• Alice follows a mysterious girl into a secret society where she experiences crazy adventures with her new friends as she seeks for a way into the group. (Note: this is the plot of my novel, ALICE IN WONDERLAND HIGH.)

• Wendy and her brothers follow a boy onto a spaceship run by kids and battle space pirates. She accepts the role of their leader and must decide if she wants to stay or leave to start her own fleet.

• Elizabeth Bennett and Mr. Darcy both come from different sides of an apocalyptic war and must overcome their biggest weaknesses—his pride in his nation, hers prejudice against his—and band together to overthrow their governments and fall in love.

• A group of clones cast off by the company who created them called The Wizard must band together and trek across dangerous lands to retrieve the missing body parts needed to make them whole again.

4. Identify what the main character in the original story wanted and come up with a parallel.

• Alice wants to get inside the beautiful garden and then go home; in my contemporary version she wants to get inside the secret society and find her home there.

• Wendy and her brothers want to remain young forever but end up growing up in the process. Maybe in the sci-fi version Wendy and her brothers join the space ship to escape their chores but end up with more.

• Dorothy wants to go home, and in this case, home might be the lab that created her but when she gets there, she realizes she belongs free of it.

• Elizabeth Bennett wants to find a man to marry, maybe in the apocalyptic version, she's fighting for her right to marry.

5. Do the same for the rest of the characters by keeping a key trait while also giving them new ones.

• The Chesire Cat is a cute boy named Chester Katz with a penchant for disappearing and a killer smile.

• Peter Pan flies a spaceship; Tinker Bell is the Siri-like computer console.

• The Scarecrow wants a brain, but maybe in the new version he wants to become sentient.

- Lydia falls for the wrong guy and gets stuck with him; maybe in the new version Lydia falls for the wrong side of the war and gets stranded there.

6. Write down two scenes from the original and figure out ways to re-set them in your version.

- Alice cries a pool of tears. Instead Alice floods the school.

- Alice rescues a pig from a cook which turns into a baby. Alice rescues a pig from a campus lab by dressing it as a baby.

You get the idea. From there keep going until you've mapped out your entire tale. And then it's just a matter of writing it!

EXERCISE #11:

Now it's your turn! Follow the steps above to create retelling concepts of your own.

Retell A Story With Another POV

WICKED by Gregory Maguire was the story of THE WIZARD OF OZ retold from the witch's POV. It took the central elements of the original: she has green skin, possesses flying monkeys, has a sister with magical shoes, and retreats to a castle. But from there Maguire re-imagined everything about the world that centered around the witch character. I'm guessing he started by asking questions. Why does the sister have those shoes but the Wicked Witch of the West does not? Why is her skin green? Why does she melt when she's doused with water and how the hell does she shower? Why does she live in a castle?

But he also answered larger questions about the world. Why do some animals talk and act like humans while others remain animals? How did the city of Oz come to be? Is she really wicked? What is her backstory like with Glinda, the Good Witch of the North?

He answered those questions and then built them out into a new story. His own story. The events of the original play out in the background late in the book. Everything on the pages of WICKED was his.

But you want to create your own. You already wrote out log lines for several stories in the previous exercise. Now choose the most interesting supporting character from those stories. Or maybe it's not the most interesting character...yet. Not until you have your way with the character.

Maybe you want to tell the dark history Tiger Lily like Jodi Lynn Anderson did in her book. Or maybe it's no one currently in the book and you're going to tell a new story. For example, in HOOK'S REVENGE, Heidi Schulz tells the story of Captain Hook's daughter. What was really going on behind quiet Kitty's eyes in PRIDE AND PREJUDICE? Perhaps she wasn't as quiet as everyone thinks. The book LONGBOURNE by Jo Baker retells PRIDE AND PREJUDICE from the perspective of the maids downstairs.

Let's take ALICE IN WONDERLAND and go through the motions. I'll list out a few of the well known side characters that could be interesting to write about.

- Queen of Hearts

- Mad Hatter

- Caterpillar

- White Rabbit

Now delve deeper for each option and write down a few central facts about them that would be interesting to explore in a full novel.

QUEEN OF HEARTS

• How did he become such a hookah addict? Where does he even get his supply?

• What happens to him after he becomes a butterfly?

I don't know about you but I'm immediately drawn to the idea of learning more about the Queen of Hearts came to despise heads with a built in romance. But of course, any idea needs conflict. We can find that by asking more questions. What does the Queen of Hearts want and what's standing in her way of getting it? Maybe her want is tied into her penchant for decapitation. Maybe she was trained as a warrior but ended up as a queen and she wants nothing more than to fight on a battlefield. Maybe she's an active hunter and she affixes the heads to her wall, dead deer style.

But we could also choose a character who doesn't quite exist yet. Let's list out a few options.

• The Mad Hatter's sister, a woman who stays sane by keeping to herself in Wonderland.

• The King of Spades, ruler of another area of Wonderland where things are even wackier than the Wonderland we know.

• Alice's sister, who appears in chapter one and never again. Maybe her sister has her own adventure that's even curiouser.

EXERCISE #12:

Your challenge is to find the most interesting perspective from the four options you chose during the previous exercise. List out all the potential character options and invent a few that don't currently exist. Write out a log line that reimagines the story from an existing supporting character for each. And then also write out a log line from the perspective of a character that's new to the world within the story. Make sure each character wants something and there's something standing in their way of getting it.

Rewriting An Existing Blurb

For this technique, you take any blurb you want to reimagine. Peruse Amazon, Goodreads, or maybe IMDB. Try to find blurbs that are short, one paragraph or less, because they are easier to work with. On IMDB, you can work with log lines and that might make things easier.

You don't have to choose anything in the Public Domain because for this exercise, you'll be changing enough elements to make your version completely different. This is just a starting point.

For the purposes of demonstration, let's twist up one of my own blurbs. Here is a short blurb for my New Adult romance, MASTER PROBATION:

To get revenge on the sexy jerk who orchestrated her sorority's demise, Bianca makes it her mission to unearth Harrison's scandalous secret. Exposing it would get Harrison's frat expelled and hers reinstated, but how can she turn him in when she's falling for him?

Now here's the blurb with the variables scrubbed out:

To get revenge on the [adjective to describe the love interest] who [what the love interest did to piss off protagonist], Bianca makes it her mission to [protagonist's goal]. [Verb] it would [consequence and outcome of goal], but how can she [dilemma] when she's falling for him?

Let's now plug in new details into the above using the romance tropes found earlier in the book. Eventually you'll change the names as well but I'm keeping them the same for demonstration purposes.

To get revenge on the [new detective] who [solved her big case before she could], Bianca makes it her mission to [one up him by solving all his cases]. [Solving] it would [make her the lead candidate for a promotion and get him sent right back to another department], but how can she [throw him under the bus] when she's falling for him?

That's a start, but maybe there are ways to further twist it and make it your own. Maybe there's a new obstacle we can add in there, an external consequence that throws a wrench in their plans. To figure out one, I start thinking of all possibilities that will work with this premise—a detective solving a case.

Chapter 7: Using Free Writing

Free writing is the act of setting a pen to paper or fingers to a keyboard and typing whatever comes to your mind. No prep work allowed. No editing as you go. No second guessing yourself.

So how does free writing help to generate ideas?

My novel, KASEY SCREWS UP THE WORLD, began as a free writing exercise. It was the first day of NaNoWriMo during my first year participating. I had decided to join the day before it started. I'd written novels before but did not currently have any shiny new book ideas screaming at me to be written. I could have stopped there, before I even started. Waved the white flag and called it a day. Nothing would have changed, I would have been in the exact same place as I was: someone still searching for her next book idea.

But just like the fear of the blank page doesn't stop me, I didn't let a pesky thing as not having a premise or any sort of plot affect me. The only thing I had was a character name—Kasey—something I picked about ten seconds before I started writing. I knew literally nothing about this character. I decided to let her show me who she was.

I set a timer for fifteen minutes. I turned off the Internet. And I just started typing. I didn't let myself stop to think. I didn't let my fingers stop typing. Any time my mind wanted to pause and think, I ignored it and just kept going. I started with dialogue, with another character asking Kasey questions. But as I typed, I realized those questions were not coming out in a nice way. They were harsh. They were abrasive. They were accusatory. And Kasey was avoiding answering them because she felt guilty.

Suddenly I had the seeds of a story. A character pissed off at Kasey, interrogating her over something she did. Something Kasey didn't want to admit.

I sat back and started to analyze what I had by asking questions. What is happening on the page currently? What could happen next? And then after that? I looked to see if there was a driving force in the novel somewhere, such as what emerged in mine: a character who pissed off others somehow and is guilt-ridden about it. What did that character do to anger others and how can she make things right again?

I kept writing. I let the characters guide me. I wrote until Kasey showed me what her secret was. Until I learned the wrongs she caused to those she loved. And then I wrote until I followed her journey while she tried to fix her mistakes.

This method is called pantsing, and I'll be the first to admit that pantsing a novel makes me uncomfortable. I didn't get very far, maybe about two chapters, in my free writing before I started shaping what I already had into an outline and envisioning future scenes before I wrote them. But that's okay. Because the point is that the initial free writing exercise is what generated the book idea for me. Once I had something on the page, I was able to see what it was and where it needed to go.

You don't need to start free writing from absolute scratch. You can choose two or three items from your Stream of Consciousness List and use those to guide you as you free write. Or maybe you simply start with the most universal premise of all: Your character has a secret. It's your job to uncover what that secret is through free writing. Don't think about it in advance. Don't incorporate any preconceived notions about your character. Just start putting words down on a page and let that secret take shape. The trick to this is to write fast and not stop until that timer goes off.

EXERCISE #15:

You have a character. That character is harboring a secret. Your job is to free write until you uncover what that secret is. Set a timer for at least fifteen minutes but no more than thirty minutes. Turn off your Internet, even if that means driving to a park somewhere with no wifi access and typing on a bench. Start writing and don't pause for even a second until that timer goes off. The only thing you are allowed to figure out in advance is the character's name. Once you've written, step back and analyze your work by asking yourself questions about it.

Alternatively, you can choose three of the items from your Stream of Consciousness List, set a timer, turn off theinternet, and free write something that incorporates all the elements from your list. Then analyze what you have.

Using What Ifs

Some authors are notorious for using what ifs to generate book ideas. What if a vampire fell in love with a human? (TWILIGHT) What if the government split the population into five factions based on people's beliefs about human virtues? (DIVERGENT) What if Harry

Potter was set in a college rather than an elementary school? (THE MAGICIANS).

In this technique, you start with a what if question. But how do you actually get a what if question? You can start by googling hypothetical questions or what ifs and see what comes up in the search results. I went to a science based hypothetical page and found some cool questions I could build stories out of:

• What if you fell into a black hole?

• What if there was no gravity?

• What if Earth's magnetic poles stopped working?

And then there were some wacky questions:

• What if all the cats in the world died at once?

• What if everyone on the planet jumped at the same time?

Or maybe you think of your own what ifs by questioning something you're interested in. To do this, let's refer back to our Stream of Consciousness List and choose two items from it. I've chosen these items from my list:

• Beer brewing

• Being snowed in

Now I'll start thinking of all types of what if questions related to those topics.

Beer brewing

• What if there was a repeat of prohibition in present day?

• What if someone figured out how to brew a secret ingredient into beer that gives people temporary super powers?

• What if someone slipped a lethal poison into a large batch of beer brewed at a huge company like Budweiser?

Being snowed in

- What if the snow never stops and starts to pile so high, you're trapped in your house?

- What if the snow turns acidic and starts eating away at the house and landscape?

- What if you're snowed in alone with your crush?

From here I eliminate the ideas that don't interest me (acidic snow, snow never stopping, repeat of prohibition) and start focusing in on ideas that interest me. I'm intrigued by am amateur brewing super power-laced beer. I'm also intrigued by getting trapped somewhere alone with your crush. That could make for a cute NA or YA novel. The beer could make for a fun adult magical novel.

The questions, as usual, come next. Where is the girl trapped with her crush? Why are they together? What is their relationship like—are they friends, enemies, thrown together on a joint project? And for the beer brewing: what kind of super powers? Who drinks the beer? How does it affect them?

I start to answer those questions until I nail down a premise with a character, a goal, and a conflict.

EXERCISE #16:

Scour the web for a what if question to answer and also choose a few items from your Stream of Consciousness List and ask strange questions about those. Then answer the questions until you figure out a new book idea.

Combining Ideas

By now you've written a lot of potential premises. Some probably sucked. Some have potential. If you haven't already come up with something that sparked you enough to start writing or outlining, then you may need a boost to get there. The next trick I have up my sleeve is to combine two ideas that aren't working on their own. The two ideas could be completely different and have nothing to do with each other. They could even be different genres. But what happens when you put them together?

This was one way I developed the plot for my Alice in Wonderland retelling ALICE IN WONDERLAND HIGH. I had two separate ideas I was mulling over. One was a non-fantasy retelling of Alice in which I had the characters but had no plot for them. I knew the Cheshire Cat would become Chester Katz, a boy with a killer smile and a penchant for disappearing. I knew Dinah the cat would become Alice's fickle best friend. The Queen of Hearts would be the queen bee of the school named Quinn Hart. But again, I had no story for these characters. I had no idea what happened once Alice followed the White Rabbit character, Whitney Lapin.

Simultaneously, I was fleshing out an idea involving two girls who infiltrate a secret society in their school but had gotten stuck after identifying the first chapter. But then I thought...what if I combine the two ideas?

Suddenly it all clicked. Alice wanted to get into a secret society. That's why she follows Whitney. That's where Chester disappears to. That's what Quinn is trying to thwart. From there I was able to create a plot.

Let's take two ideas we've already created during the exercises and try to combine them into something new.

• She inherited an estate belonging to the dead relative and either has to clean it out or she makes it her new residence. It resides in a quirky seaside town that's very different from her big city life.

• Invitation into a fictional Bilderberg meeting falls into the wrong hands

So we've got a girl that inherits an estate from a dead relative—maybe the dad she hadn't spoken to in years—and travels there to clean it out. She discovers an invitation to a very secret world leader meeting. Yet here she thought her dad held a blue collar job. She decides to attend the meeting but learns of its sinister agenda.

Here is another example:

• What if you're snowed in alone with your crush?

• A girl on the run through time after escaping a time travel cult is being pursued by the sadistic cult leader.

So we've got a girl running through time. And then a scenario in which she's snowed in with her crush. If we combine these two, it might help identify who she is and what her plan is. She's not just escaping from the time travel cult. She's escaping to meet a boy she's forbidden to meet. Maybe the cult strictly forbids relations of any kind with people from other time periods because of the ripple effect it could cause on the world. Maybe the cult doesn't just worship time travel but they consider themselves protectors of history, so by falling for someone she shouldn't, she's directly disobeying their orders. If she escapes, the first place she'd likely run is to her crush, who lives in 2249. She's just made it to the woods behind his house when the cult leader catches up to her. In a daring escape, she grabs the hand of her crush and whisks him away to a new time period to hide out. Maybe it's a ski lodge in the 1930s. Maybe it's a cave covered in snow in the prehistoric era. Either way, they hide out there and when she thinks it's safe and goes to leave, she realizes she no longer has the ability to time travel. The cult has turned it off and restricted her access. They're trapped during a huge snow storm and now they're sitting ducks. Oh and even worse? He had no idea she could time travel.

EXERCISE #17:

Take two of the ideas you worked out on the other pages and try to combine them. Let go of any parts of the idea that don't fit in the new version. Expand on what you already have. If the combined ideas still don't work, try again.

Part 5:

FLESHING OUT YOUR IDEAS

Fleshing Out Your Ideas

So you've got a few working idea options that intrigue you. But how do you turn the basics of an idea (character, goal, conflict) into a full plot? How do you even know which idea has legs? How do you go from idea to project?

Over the next few pages, I'll be laying out techniques to help you answer every question!

Creating Pitches To Weed Out Ideas

The first step in determining whether an idea has legs or not is to create a longer pitch blurb. A longer pitch blurb is the same as you might see on the back of a book in a book store. It's about two paragraphs long and it's written in a way to hook readers. It usually has a cliffhanger ending or ends on some kind of intriguing unanswered question designed to lure someone into reading the book. For those familiar with the process to acquire a literary agent, these can also be called query pitches.

Chances are, if you're writing a novel, you want to do something with it. Maybe that something is to try to snag an agent and sell it to a traditional publisher. Maybe that something is to self-publish it and sell it online. In both scenarios, you'll eventually need a blurb, so my feeling is you have nothing to lose in creating one before you start writing. You can always tweak it later if it doesn't match up after you finish.

Pitch blurbs are especially great at exposing low stakes (where there isn't anything dire driving the events of the story) or lack of character goals (the character doesn't seem to want anything) or lack of conflict (nothing is standing in the character's way of getting what they want) or lack of a plot (the events that start off the premise don't seem to go anywhere). I find it works best for me to write several pitch blurbs of different ideas in a row. The first one starts off as a difficult task but by the time I get to the third or so, I can more easily knock them out. Once I write the blurb, it immediately starts to become clear that the premise isn't working...or alternatively, that it is.

Before you start writing pitches from scratch, you may want to practice writing blurbs so you know what makes a good one and what makes a bad one.

I have two methods for practicing.

1. Take a book you know very well and write a pitch blurb for it as it might appear on the back of the book. Once you're done, check your work against the real blurb. Compare what details you put in there versus what details they did. Compare wording choice. Then do this several more times with other books.

2. Critique other people's blurbs. Once you can start identifying what doesn't work in someone else's blurb, you'll have an easier

time identifying what doesn't work in your own. Absolutewrite.com and Critiquecircle.com are two sites with forums where people can post blurbs for critique. Head over there and start critiquing until you have a pretty good idea of the components for a good pitch.

Once you've got a handle on how to write a great blurb, it's time to start fleshing your log lines into paragraphs.

I'm going to take one of the first log lines we created when using the X meets Y method: The Skulls meets Midnight in Paris. A girl receives a weird invitation into a secret society that exists only in the past.

As I mentioned previously, this is an idea I've already written, but it all started with the log line. From there, I started asking myself questions and then answering them to figure out some more information.

Who is the main character and how would a secret society invitation affect her?

- A girl who is an outcast in her school as well as at home due to her parents' re-marriages. She feels like she has nowhere she truly belongs. Until she receives the invitation. Maybe this could be the one place she feels at home.

What about the secret society makes her feel like she belongs there if it's set in the past?

- Maybe she meets a boy from the past who shares her own passions and fears.

- Maybe the most popular boy from present day receives an invitation too and they start to bond about their journey.

Why does the secret society need to be set in the past?

- Maybe there's some mystery they need to solve for the secret society using some skills only they possess.

- Maybe members from the future of the Main Character's timeline also attend the meetings, so the attendees are from all over time.

• Maybe there is something strange about the building the meetings are being held in that bends time.

What is the main conflict?

• The longer she stays in the past, the more out of touch with her own reality she becomes.

• The link starts closing and she must solve a mystery before it does.

• Other kids from her school find the link and start infiltrating the society.

Once I have a bunch of answers to the questions, I try to put it in a blurb. I always start with character in these blurbs. So I've got a girl that feels like an outcast at school and at home. I start by plugging in some variables to make that true. I also pick a placeholder name for the character. I don't spend too much time obsessing over this. I can change it later. I don't fret too much over word choice but I've written so many blurbs now that they naturally come out voicey in first drafts. It's okay if they're not at this stage.

This is what I get when I start plugging in variables:

Seventeen-year-old Rory not only feels like an outcast in her school, she feels like an impostor in her own life. Her parents are both re-married with brand new families and babies, forcing her to shuffle between them like the alimony checks that used to arrive. They act like she's a guest in their homes instead of someone who belongs. At school, she's been kicked out of as many cliques as she has clubs.

Okay, that's pretty good set up for the character. We know what she wants: to belong. We know why she hasn't found a place she belongs yet.

Now we need to introduce the catalyst, the invitation she receives that ultimately leads into the past. I also like to add something about what the character might be giving up in order to follow the catalyst. This helps to amp the stakes. If the character received the invitation and was like, "okay great!" that's not very good conflict. So I pondered ways in which receiving an invitation might generate conflict. Maybe she doesn't believe it's real and instead thinks it's a practical joke put on her by the classmates that treat her horribly. If that's the case though, why would she actually do what the invitation says? Maybe if she plans to retaliate by pulling one over on the very people she thinks are pranking her. So from there we get the next few lines:

So when she receives an invitation in her locker to what appears to be a secret society initiation, she assumes it's a joke on her behalf. She decides to stay one move ahead and concocts an plan to catch them in the act and expel someone else for once. But when she sneaks into the school basement in the middle of the night for the initiation, she's transported to the past MIDNIGHT IN PARIS-style and finds what she hadn't bargained for: acceptance.

At this point we need to introduce the reason for her to stay (or at least the reason for her to keep going back into the society) as well as the main conflict of the story. And I want to end up something intriguing, some kind of cliffhanger or unanswered question. I start plugging in a few of the answers to the questions above to see what works. Here is version 1:

There she meets an enigmatic boy who lives in the 1920s who shares her passions and her fears. Each night she returns for another pledge task and each day she resumes her own reality, which she slowly loses touch with. But the past and present collide when a mystery unravels that only she can solve using clues gleamed from both timelines. If she solves it, she'll save the lives of every society member from all timelines, but she'll also close the link to the past, leaving her with nothing but the life she left behind.

But I also liked the idea that the boy she meets is from present day because there might be a better resolution to the romance if they are from the same time period. So I plug different variables in for version 2:

But she's not alone. The most popular boy in school, Griffin, receives a similar invitation and the two bond with both each other and the other members of the secret society. Rory learns she and Griffin have more in common than she ever thought, and he seems like he could become not only an ally but a friend. But the next day, Griffin ignores her as if the whole experience never happened, leading Rory to worry it was all in her mind. Each night the two return to the secret society and experience the fun of the 1920s before they resume the drear of their current lives. Soon the link between the past and the present blurs with more of Rory's high school enemies infiltrating the secret society in the past and with aspects of the past showing up in her every day life. She and Griffin must work together to close the link before they lose all sense of which reality is which and where they belong.

Now I have two different versions. Both have pros and cons. I like the mystery aspect of version one, but I also like the romance better in version two. Maybe I can combine some elements of both versions to create version 3.

But she's not alone. The most popular boy in school, Griffin, receives a similar invitation and the two bond with both each other and the other members of the secret society. Rory learns she and Griffin have more in common than she ever thought, and he seems like he could become not only an ally but a friend. But the next day, Griffin ignores her as if the whole experience never happened, leading Rory to worry it was all in her mind. Until the past and present collide when a mystery unravels that only they can solve using clues gleamed from both timelines. Each night the two return to the secret society to gather more clues before they resume the drear of their current lives. Soon the link between the past and the present blurs with more of Rory's high school enemies infiltrating the secret society in the past and with aspects of the past showing up in her every day life. She and Griffin must work together to solve the mystery and close the link before the mystery claims their very lives.

Ah! There. Now we've got lots of conflict, life and death stakes, a romance with a clear arc, and story that seems like it can fill a whole plot. Together it looks like:

Seventeen-year-old Rory not only feels like an outcast in her school, she feels like an impostor in her own life. Her parents are both re-married with brand new families and babies, forcing her to shuffle between them like the alimony checks that used to arrive. They act like she's a guest in their homes instead of someone who belongs. At school, she's been kicked out of as many cliques as she has clubs.

But she's not alone. The most popular boy in school, Griffin, receives a similar invitation and the two bond with both each other and the other members of the secret society. Rory learns she and Griffin have more in common than she ever thought, and he seems like he could become not only an ally but a friend. But the next day, Griffin ignores her as if the whole experience never happened, leading Rory to worry it was all in her mind. Until the past and present collide when a mystery unravels that only they can solve using clues gleamed from both timelines. Each night the two return to the secret society to gather more clues before they resume the drear of their current lives. Soon the link between the past and the present blurs with more of Rory's high school enemies infiltrating the secret society in the past and with aspects of the past showing up in her every day life. She and Griffin must work together to solve the mystery and close the link before the mystery claims their very lives.

The next step is to do this with all your promising ideas. I like to do this in batches of ten. As soon as I get stuck on something and can't figure out a good way to add more tension, stakes, or conflict, I nix it or try it another way. Once I have ten that seem to work, I can usually narrow down to about five, nixing the ones that either don't interest me or don't seem as cool as the others. Then I usually send the ideas to a trusted critique partner or my agent to help me decide what to write next.

And once I know which one I'll be writing, I start to mull over individual scenes.

Setting Your Mindset

You love to write! But you've found yourself wracking your head on how to put the thoughts down. You started off with a paragraph and you have watch time drift away with nothing else resurrecting, then you decided to cool off with watching the TV. At other points you would search pages of a book to pick ideas that could help and found yourself rampaging the whole book and wasting your time. You took the time to research and then you took the whole day to write nothing. It may also be that sleep came and drift you away from all your troubles, and you found rest in doing nothing. This is all part of the struggle. Don't stop. Just write.

With the help of this book, you'll do all the painstaking, tough practice of unlearning those bad habits and beliefs of yours that gets to your way of higher skill.

Writing seems to be a hard thing, even harder in a noisy world full of blaring distractions, financial pressures, success envy, and scary things like author lawsuits. It can be easy to give up before you get started. The Noise that has the highest potential to drown you is the noise in your head and you are the only one to stop the way against it.

Distractions come in 3 packages:

The Pressure to Make Money. The quest to earn money and more money is too often the number 1 distractions writers face. You can overcome that if you know the game well. First of all, do you want to make your writer choices based on succeeding as a writer, or how much you'll earn? This options maybe too hard for some because there's a greater need for financial security. Not to worry, you can climb the ladder of being a successful writer while putting away thousands of $$$ from the contest you won. The debate in the later chapters of this book will teach you how easy and glaring it is before your own eyes. So, just don't call it quits – you're actually quite creative!

The Rise of Social Media. The explosion of marketing advertising and showbiz can be a little more catastrophic than promotional. Don't get me wrong, it does well to those at the top where their names, books, and videos are promoted and sold; but the unintended consequences for the starters is that they take the whole time exploring and many times lose their way...and take a long time to come back. It can be hard to navigate. You may not want to be overwhelmed, but browsing all of this various information will do just that. There is far too information out there and you can't digest all at the same time. Sometimes all you need is a solitary reflection, a simple image before you, a sentence to expand, and a pen and paper to just write.

The Fear of Criticism. Everyone hopes for their craft to be appreciated. There's fear of what would be people's reactions. This fear is more apt for emerging writers and has a way of turning good writers into people pleasers. If care is not taken, the effect would be losing your voice and not writing your full story. Absorbing critique and negative feedback can skew your thoughts, whether you're a beginner or top notch. Don't let people's judgment play on the background of your creativity. You can listen to gain the reasonableness of their ideas, but never be deafened by the sound of wrong ideas.

Now having said that, it's good to know that your mind has been given the freedom to venture into the world of storytelling. Raising your eyebrows? Yes freedom is all you need to start. I, as a writer, happened to break away from the fear of criticism. It was after I wrote my first story, which was children's fiction, that I discovered my writing skills had unfolded. I had another story idea that I passionately wanted to write and publish, but fear restricted me from taking the right steps forward. I was afraid that I will be judged for touching matters in which I have no experience with. I was afraid that I haven't a degree in creative writing and that it will be a problem writing a story for adults, so, I kept the idea and enrolled into a course in creative writing. I was afraid that the political parts of my story might stir some violence against me. With all these alarming fears, I drifted back to the edge of myself. Not until I talked to a publishing company at Singapore that wanted to help me publish and market my children's story did I realize how much of my legs were at other people's field instead of mine. I have given my time to acquire another degree not because it's a criterion but because I wanted critics to not be able to bring me down.

The craft of writing unfolds with the many efforts you put into writing; reading, doing what you love, traveling, taking down thoughts and observations and the rest of it which will get deeper into later in this book.

Before anything else, I have two bits of advice to offer you now. They are:

- Be Inspired, Always. There's this aging belief that there must be a grievous event that instigated the art of writing in every successful writer. The instances given could be abuse, bullying, hardship, war, natural disaster, death of a loved one, and so on. This is true. But many writers will not admit theirs. I don't expect them to. Is hard to admit anyways. It may not be so for some writers though. Now, if pains can propel people to write and you were fortunate to have such a pain-free life, there is something you must do. Leave that comfort zone; it's time to take a stroll. Try to discover what matters to you, find ideas to challenge, look for problems to solve, understand the norms of a society that seem strange to you. Doing this and doing it passionately can give you a good story to write.

- Take Your Time. This is especially for writers who have gained some experiences. At times, all you need is to close the book and retrieve to living your life, observing life and people, maybe with a few days of solitude, travelling, and meeting new people. This will reintroduce you to your core values as a writer or can cause a long overdue confrontation.

Chapter 8: Getting Moving

You may have heard the saying that "every writer is a good reader". Let me tell you that that's just the preamble to the practice of writing. It's time to kill the struggle. Let's do it!

Read! Nothing can ignite the sparkle of your writing more than reading. Read widely, from scientific theories to political objectives, and variety of stories. "Read when you feel like reading, read when you don't feel like reading, read until you feel like reading. If you have taken initiative from the advice given above – "be inspired", and if you have chosen one of the things that matters to you to write then you have to do this also: read those books that have similar voices with yours, reread them and also reread those books that made you fall in love with expression and storytelling.

Stop Reading! Calm down -- before you freak out, reading is still where it's at. A lot of authors admitted that reading varieties of books when they are in the middle of writing their story can distract them. Since what we read influences us, reading wildly can mess up the sound of our own voice when we are just putting it down.

Don't over think! Thinking is great but thinking too much is a form of procrastination. It is a product of fear and doubt. Deep down, you already know what you want to write, put it on the paper, it is called first draft; you can edit it later, as often as you want.

Tone up! Along that line, try holding a conversation about the subject you're writing and see what the people around you have to say. Ask questions. Asking questions and learning their answers helps you to contrast the differences in your ideas and strengthen some of your doubts.

Ask yourself these important questions. You need to start by asking yourself these four critical questions: Who is my audience and what is the message I want to share with them? What emotion do I intend to rouse in my audience? What is the core moral that I want to impact in my readers? Can I summarize my intent as one sentence or word? First settle with the idea of your story before setting off on how best to convey it.

Invent from your experiences. Your experiences; happy or painful are tools through which you can build your career, establish your brand, or tell your story. There's a saying that, "how you navigate through your problems can equate who you are." For storytelling it can also equate your voice. There's an event in your life that propels the idea you're trying to share. Stories that entails struggles, pains, and how you climb to success are not easy to be forgotten by readers

Highlight a challenge. A story without a challenge simply isn't complete, even comedies dramas have their struggles. A Good storyteller understands that a story needs conflict. Could be conflict in a place, of a people, or you can cue in something from your own life struggles. Don't be afraid to suggest new ideas or challenge old convictions.

Keep it simple. You don't need to prove yourself with big vocabulary and grammar. Stories require simplicity and expression. Work from principles you learn from this book. You can lay emphasis when there's need to and not because you wish to spice up your ideas.

Be consistent. Practice makes perfect. Storytelling is as an art that demands consistency. You need to be on the move. Widen your horizon. After you analyze yourself and found you're becoming better, the next thing up is to upgrade the books you read. Reading is your lifestyle. Similar as you would upgrade your wardrobe, you have to spontaneously upgrade your library. Encode your communication; when with colleagues, hone your conversation into the most effective and efficient story. You're practicing, remember. The rewards can be immense. So, for the extra three minutes you spend encoding a leadership communication in a story, you're going to see returns that last for months and maybe even years.

3

The Four Essentials of Storytelling

The four essentials of storytelling – Dialogue, Setting, Character and Voice are interactive arts that sunders utterly in time and space. These are the principles required of you to write your story.

Meaning Beyond The Margin

1.   Dialogue. There is dialogue in both speaking and writing. Dialogue is a face to face interaction between persons (characters) who fill the space between expression and emotion. It is linked by many threads on communication such as senses and movements. Each emotion your story portrays is a sense of judgment in that space between your voice and your characters

voices. Voice carries an intimate message of emotions, tone, rhythms, impulse, intentions, memory, and beliefs. As tangible as stories may to seem be, it can be meaningful, or dismissed by the readers who are in the world of the interaction. By enlightening you on this, it is not to absolve you into a scholarly prejudice, rather, it is for you to trace the borders of your discipline and your audience and create the chat of your characters in written words

2. Setting. A setting is as alive as characters in your book. It has heart and soul, moods and influence on the events of your story and on the readers. You need to give much ardor to constructing your setting the same way you do with characters. It is important that you know and understand the setting of your story as ideally as you know your own neighborhood. You have the option to use a real setting or a fictional one.

Now let's get deeper. How much details to add to the setting of your story is up to you.

Some folks like to paint an elaborate image, that's great. It's also great to do very little. It's just like choice of spices you prefer for your food. But when you have a voluminous book in mind you need to widen your creative flow in describing your setting.

In my stories, I give the credit of my settings to quality than quantity. When you know the most appropriate names in the register to describe your settings there's no need to waste your time painting a huge picture. Setting not only includes the main location but the wider geography. Take for example: "Steve went to swim in a river." Yes we understand that the character "Steve" happened to go to a swimming game on a river, there may be the need to tell us where the river is located, the things surrounding the river, or anything else. Something like: Steve went to swim on the river at the outskirts of town." It all depends on the imagination you want to create. You need to make the settings of your story interesting or unusual. Great writers give style and sensibility to their settings. Settings also include the history and customs of the people or your characters. One can fall in love with your setting just by how well you crafted it. And is a good thing to know that you need no superior knowledge to craft a breathtaking setting, a little insider knowledge and your creative juice can do the job for you.

Like this piece here:

"This place reminds me of how technology can ally with nature to create a wonder. Some centuries ago, this was void, until the vision came. Is just amazing looking out on the blue sea and again raising your head up to be greeted by the friendly blue sky. The bridge in the centre of the water here is a function of technology working together with nature. Is amazing isn't it?"

You can also go beyond the concrete to the abstract in describing settings. Some abstracts like weather, smell, or a natural disaster. Just anything that goes beyond the physical geography.

3. Characters. While dialogues and settings are important, Character is the tool to create relationship in your story. Before you begin your characterization, consider the categories of relationship you want to create. Employ introspection; as a way to develop your character relationships. Make your characters think or exhibit an emotion with their bonds. Emotions like love, hate, doubt fear, etc. use introspective scenes to harness your style and evolve round your main character and the other characters. Take some events to tell your readers who your characters are, their intentions, passion thoughts, strength, weakness and many more. Your character can be typical, unique, universal or allegorical. Make your character feel plausible by expressing their ideas and the way they look. Is your character tall? Does she have a blue eyes and the sound of her voice, when you describe things this way you draw readers to create the reality and picture of your story in their mind.

4. Voice. There are couple ways to portray voice in a story. There is author voice and main character voice. Voice is how you speak and think and how you put it in black and white. Everyone has their unique voice unless you consciously and constantly pay attention to someone else's voice instead of your own. Character voice on the other hand is your invention to portray who your character is. If you want to write a story with strong voice, use the first person or third person narrative. Usually the first is more effective to create a transparent voice. There is also a second person narrative voice but this is difficult to apply and it's rarely used. Readers mostly expect a first or third person viewpoint.

In my stories, I try to use dialect, accent, slangs rhythm, and other flavors to highlight the educational background, status, and the voice of my character.

4

Practical Ingredients

It's time we look at the four essential story ingredients that will make our story great.

1. Orientation. The beginning of your story must be attention grabbing. It should welcome the reader into your curb. You can achieve this with describing your setting as remarkable, create a mood, bring in a tone, and as you go down the line you introduce your protagonist creating an aura for him or her. This is important. If readers don't pay attention to your protagonist, it'll be hard for them to finish your story.

2. Crisis. Just like in real word, eventually, there will be ups and down in the life of your protagonist or other character. Crisis is unavoidable; it helps set the plot and characterization in your story. The imbalances (crisis) may happen as a backstory before the story begins, but you should at least let one happen in the development of your plot. The crisis that alters your character's life might be a call to adventure that leads to fulfillment, a tragedy that unfolds the real world, a quest

that could make or break him or a revelation that will clear his doubts. Crisis creates a turning point in your story. Examples: Emily got divorced, Sandra suffered heartbreak, and Ford had an accident.

3.   Discovery. At the climax of the crisis in the life of the protagonist, there should be a discovery that helps him transcend his crisis. The protagonist discovery may come by the choice he makes or by chance this usually depends on the kind of story and writer's perspective. Let your story be a paradox of what the readers will most likely predict as the end of your story. It will thrill the reader more when the story ends unpredictably and satisfying.

4.   Change. Even if your story idea comes from space there will still be a change or transformation that streamlines the reality or myth of your story. Though the genre of your story can dictate the direction of your transformation. for Romance, it could be reconciliation. For horror stories it may end

with the death of the villain. This is used to create emotional healing or awakening from one emotion to another.

www.ingramcontent.com/pod-product-compliance
Lightning Source LLC
Chambersburg PA
CBHW050024130526
44590CB00042B/1901